Scottish Political Parties and the 2014 Independence Referendum

Scottish Political Parties and the 2014 Independence Referendum

Kevin Adamson & Peter Lynch

Welsh Academic Press
Cardiff

Published in Wales by Welsh Academic Press, an imprint of

Ashley Drake Publishing Ltd
PO Box 733
Cardiff
CF14 7ZY

www.welsh-academic-press.com

First Edition – 2014

ISBN
978-1-86057-121-3

© Ashley Drake Publishing Ltd 2014
Text © Peter Lynch 2014

The right of Kevin Adamson & Peter Lynch to be identified as the author of this work has been asserted in accordance with the Copyright Design and Patents Act of 1988.

All rights reserved. No part of this publication may be reproduced, stored in a retrieval system, or transmitted, in any form or by any means without the prior permission of the publishers.

British Library Cataloguing-in-Publication Data.
A CIP catalogue for this book is available from the British Library.

Typeset by Replika Press Pvt Ltd, India
Printed by

Contents

List of Contributors 7

Preface 9

1. Introduction 1
   Scottish Political Parties and the 2014 Independence Referendum
   Kevin Adamson and Peter Lynch

2. Referendums and Sovereignty 22
   Matt Qvortrup

3. The Scottish National Party and the 2014 Independence Referendum 36
   Kevin Adamson and Peter Lynch

4. The Scottish Labour Party and the 2014 Independence Referendum 58
   Eric Shaw

5. The Scottish Conservatives and the 2014 Independence Referendum 80
   David Torrance

6. The Scottish Liberal Democrats and the 2014 Independence Referendum 101
   Malcolm Harvey

7. The Radical Parties and Independence: Another World is Possible? 125
   Paul Gillen

8. Conclusion 148
   Scottish Political Parties and the 2014 Independence Referendum
   Kevin Adamson and Peter Lynch

List of Contributors

Kevin Adamson is a lecturer in politics at the University of Stirling. His research interests are currently focused on Scottish and European politics, particularly with regard to citizenship, political ideologies and analysis of political discourse. He has published research in *Nations and Nationalism*, *East European Politics and Societies* and *Journal of Political Ideologies*

Paul Gillen is a PhD student at the University of Stirling undertaking discourse analysis on the Scottish independence referendum.

Malcolm Harvey has degrees from Stirling and Aberystywth and is completing a PhD at the University of Stirling on Scottish and Welsh governments and constitutional policy 2007-2011. He is a researcher on the ESRC programme on *Constitutional Futures and Models of Policy-Making* at the University of Aberdeen.

Peter Lynch is a Senior lecturer in Politics at the University of Stirling and Director of the Scottish Political Archive. He is author of *SNP: The Scottish National Party* [Welsh Academic Press, 2013].

Matt Qvortrup is a Senior lecturer at Cranfield University and author of *Direct Democracy: A Comparative Study of the Theory and Practice of Government by the People* [Manchester University Press, 2013] and editor of *Nationalism, Referendums and Democracy: Voting on Ethnic Issues and Independence* [Routledge, 2013].

Eric Shaw is a Senior lecturer in Politics at the University of Stirling and author of *Losing Labour's Soul* (Routledge, 2008] and co-author of *The Strange Death of Labour Scotland* [Edinburgh University Press, 2012].

David Torrance is a journalist and author of *The Battle for Britain* [Biteback, 2013], *Salmond: Against the Odds* [Birlinn, 2011] and editor of *Whatever Happened to Tory Scotland?* [Edinburgh University Press, 2012].

Preface

This book is the product of a one-day conference on political parties and the independence referendum held at the University of Stirling on 20th June 2013. The challenge for the participants and for the various authors here was to interpret an ongoing political event – the independence referendum – in mid-stream. The referendum was Scotland's third constitutional referendum since 1979 but also the longest running political campaign most of us have ever known. The conference and chapters were completed over the summer of 2013 for an event to be held on 18th September 2014. Therefore it is a book completed in mid-campaign without knowledge of the result or the last months of intense campaigning. However, the umbrella campaign groups Yes Scotland and Better Together were formally launched in May and June 2012 and the rules and procedures around the referendum itself and the campaign were known before the book was written. The Edinburgh Agreement set out the principles of the referendum in October 2012 and the Electoral Commission determined most of the details of the referendum in January 2013.

Therefore, the campaigns and the rules were established before we embarked upon this project. However, that's not to say that the campaigns or parties took active steps to engage in the campaign from the off. Rather, as the various chapters demonstrate, there was variable engagement in the campaign by the parties, all of whom were faced by the challenge of a very long campaign and the problems of contacting voters, raising funds, establishing local campaign groups and managing activists over two and a half years. The campaign was not all about issues of organization and mobilization though, it was also about devolution policy and also political discourse, in the manner in which the various political actors contested the meanings of independence, the Union, devolution, etc., as well as the meanings of welfare, society, the environment, etc. All of the party chapters examined political discourse during the campaign, employing the Essex school of discourse analysis in a common framework.

The editors would like to thank all the authors who contributed to this volume as well as to Welsh Academic Press for their agreement to publish this volume. We'd also like to thank to Andrea Baumeister, Head of the Division of History and Politics for the Division's support for the conference and also to Sarah Bromage of the Scottish Political Archive for her assistance with the conference and with collecting material on the referendum through the SPA project which can be viewed at: http://www.flickr.com/photos/scottishpoliticalarchive/

Kevin Adamson and Peter Lynch,
University of Stirling,
January 2014.

1

Introduction

Scottish Political Parties and the 2014 Independence Referendum

Kevin Adamson and Peter Lynch

Introduction

The stunning success of the Scottish National Party at the Scottish election of 2011 was the trigger for the Scottish independence referendum of 18th September 2014. The SNP achieved a majority of the seats in the Scottish Parliament and, following negotiations with the UK Government it set out plans to hold a single-question referendum on independence. What followed was an extremely long campaign – which ran from the launch of Yes Scotland on 26th May 2012 to referendum day itself. The campaign saw the construction of two umbrella campaign groups – Yes Scotland and Better Together – that acted as coordination bodies for the political parties involved in the referendum, but they also sought to establish their own offices, funding and grassroots networks. Through national and local campaigning and extensive use of social media, each umbrella group took on some 'party-like' characteristics alongside the parties as they attempted to recruit party and non-party supporters alike, to active roles in the organizations. The two groups also replicated the regular campaign repertoires of political parties – with leafleting, information stalls, public meetings and doorstep canvassing. The extent to which they were able to emerge as organizations independent of the parties – through mobilizing new activists and supporters – was questionable though, as party organization and party activists remained the backbones of the two umbrella groups throughout the long referendum campaign as well as being the political directors of the campaign groups through management boards and staffing.

Of course, without political parties, there would be no independence referendum at all. The issue of independence was driven by the Scottish National Party at a number of elections over time and, when that party entered government office in both 2007 and 2011, the issue stepped up several gears. Government office in the Scottish devolved parliament was key to the SNP's strategy for independence. Prior to devolution in 1999, the SNP had sought to win a majority of Scottish seats at Westminster and use that as a mandate for independence. However, the Scotland Act 1998 created a new institutional structure for the party to utilise. After this time, the party sought to win votes and seats in the Scottish Parliament and use that as a political and institutional platform to hold an independence referendum. This strategy enabled the party to decouple voting SNP from independence as it made independence much less immediate as the party proposed to hold the referendum in the latter stages of a Scottish parliamentary term. The SNP's main campaign themes at Scottish elections came to involve policies for economic development, education, health, local government, etc., as well as the constitutional issue, with the SNP gaining success as a policy party marginally in 2007 and then spectacularly in 2011 when it benefited from incumbency. Government office brought the independence referendum to life and meant the SNP as a party and a government had to form a Yes campaign and cooperate with others in the campaign. A similar, less ideologically-cohesive No campaign emerged through the efforts of the Conservatives, Labour and Liberal Democrats. How the various parties dealt with this new reality will be examined in the various chapters in this book.

Why Parties Matter

Despite evidence of the decline of political parties across many industrial democracies [Mair 2013], political parties have a key role in democratic politics as well as multiple functions in political systems. They serve to aggregate and articulate interests, link citizens to political institutions, educate voters, simplify choices for voters, train political elites and mobilize political issues into political institutions [see the comprehensive list of functions in Key 1965; Lawson 1988; Dalton and Wattenberg 2002]. However, they also have a key role to play in referendums at different levels. In the UK, political parties as governments are the instigators of referendums. In other political systems such as Switzerland or the United States, citizens or interest groups can play a role in generating referendums and can heavily influence the campaign at all levels. But in the UK, it is parties and governments that choose the topics, propose the questions and rules and control the referendum process. In addition, the parties are central to almost all aspects of the referendum campaign, even when there are well-funded umbrella campaigning groups on either side of a referendum question. For example, whilst much of the overt campaigning at the independence referendum involved the umbrella campaign groups Yes Scotland and Better Together, political parties remained central to the campaign at every level in political institutions, in the media and on the ground in grassroots campaigning. At some referendums, umbrella campaign groups exist as limited organizations that focus on developing cross-party cooperation and political communication: in this sense their *ad hoc* nature may make them appear as empty vessels compared to parties. However, the 2014 Scottish referendum experience was different due to the length of the campaign period – 28 months – and the manner in which each umbrella group tried to establish their own grassroots networks alongside the political parties on the ground.

There are a number of reasons why parties are central to referendum campaigning. First, there are organizational reasons. At the outset of the referendum campaign and for its duration, the political parties offered organization, staff, campaign experience, resources in terms of finance and activists on the ground and also political leadership. Second, the parties brought office benefits to the table at the referendum. They offered key supporting activities associated with government in terms of legislation, set-piece debates, critical interventions, research and reports so that some of the raw materials for the long referendum campaign originated in the two different governments through the efforts of politicians and civil servants. Third, the parties and their leading figures were major producers of political discourse throughout the campaign, in an attempt to frame the independence debate and structure political issues to suit their constitutional preference. Fourth, we can see the role of parties in generating 'campaign effects' that shaped the debate and the outcome of the referendum. For example, the popularity or unpopularity of political parties and their leaders was important to the campaign as assets to be utilized or problems to be managed.

Fifth, research has drawn attention to the role of parties in providing political cues to voters at referendums to help them navigate around the issues. According to Zaller [1992], whilst voters may or may not have strong opinions on the issue at stake at a referendum, parties will provide important cues to voters about whether to support an issue or not as voters ask 'what does my party say about this?' Of course, set against the partisan-cue factor is the decline in partisan loyalties amongst voters across Western democracies [Dalton 2013], where voters do not exhibit strong party preferences and are more open to being swayed by the campaign and by local campaign efforts and targeting [Denver and Hands 1997; Johnston and Pattie, 2010]. For example, at the 2010 UK election, only 11 per cent of voters strongly identified with political parties [Heath 2010: 124] and 46 per cent of voters were undecided at the start of the campaign proper [Green 2010: 46]. At the Scottish election of 2011, 56 per cent of voters identified with a political party – meaning almost half didn't – and even so, significant numbers either deserted their preferred party or didn't vote at all [Johns, Mitchell and Carman 2013: 160]. So, whilst parties are important in many ways at referendums, there needs to be a note of caution about partisan cues and the effectiveness of parties as mobilizing forces. As we shall see, both of these contrasting factors are influential in equal measure given the divided nature of the Scottish electorate's support for parties and evidence of partisan dealignment.

Peter Mair's work on party organization brought him to differentiate between three distinct levels of party organization: the party in public office, the party in central office and the party in the country [Mair 1994: 4]. In this book we shall endeavor to examine how parties operate at each of these levels when it comes to the referendum. The parties not only face a multi-level electoral dimension that require consideration and careful party management in the context of the referendum, but also different organizational levels of the parties face challenges in operating in a referendum. How do parties in government deal with the referendum compared to party officials and political communications staff as well as ordinary members and activists on the ground – the ordinary party workers responsible for delivering leaflets, canvassing and running the local organizations that comprise Yes Scotland and Better Together?

The Party System in Scotland and the United Kingdom

The Scottish independence referendum campaign occurred within very specific economic, political and social contexts and such contexts were influential in shaping the nature of the campaign, the different referendum coalitions and messages. The political context was shaped by the existence of political institutions, preferences and the nature of party politics in Scotland and the UK. An understanding of the party system at the Scottish and UK levels is an important starting point to explain the role of parties during the referendum campaign as well as the nature of partisan alignments during the campaign.

For example, when looking at the Scottish level of electoral politics, we can identify four distinct features that differ markedly from the UK. First, there is the existence of a more multi-party political system in Scotland, resulting from the Scottish parliament electoral system as well as voter preferences. Broader party representation has been encouraged by the fact that the electoral system involves 56 MSPs out of 129 who can be elected from regional party lists. This situation was most evident in the 2003-7 parliament, when 15 regional MSPs from three small parties plus independents were elected. However, at all elections, there is fairer representation across the political parties as votes and seats are spread across the four main parties. Second, since devolution began, Scotland has experienced two coalition governments [1999-2003 and 2003-7], followed by a minority SNP administration [2007-11] and then a SNP majority administration from 2011 onwards. Third, alongside the multi-party reality of Scottish electoral competition and representation, Scottish elections have tended to be cast as a two-party contest between Labour and the SNP. This situation may have been inevitable as these have been the two biggest parties at Scottish elections, competing for power and challenging each other's electorates over policies and political values. Since its inception, devolution elevated the SNP's political status by making it the main opposition party at Holyrood from 1999-2007 and, when the tables turned and it entered government, Labour became the main opposition [See table 1.1]. Of course, at Westminster elections, the situation was very different, with Labour clearly ahead of all other parties. [see table 1.2]

A fourth and important feature of the Scottish party system is worth mentioning, not least for its structuring effect on electoral and referendum politics: the unpopularity of the Conservatives.[1] The Conservative Party was popular in the old two-party politics of post-WW2 Scotland but declined with the rise of the Liberals and the SNP from the 1960s and then Labour successes from 1987. The Conservatives experienced serious declines in support in 1987 and 1997 [it lost all its Scottish MPs in 1997] and, whilst devolution delivered it representation at Holyrood through the regional party lists, its performance was very limited. At the Scottish election of 2011, the party achieved a record low of 13.9 per cent of the constituency vote and 11 per cent of the regional list vote. Moreover, related to this level of electoral performance, the Conservatives maintained a rather toxic status within Scottish politics for both historical and contemporary reasons. The Conservatives are somewhat akin to the concept of the 'truncated party' in Scotland [Thorlakson 2009]. The party is represented at both the regional and

Table 1.1 Scottish Election Results 1999-2011

Year	Conservative		Labour		Lib Dem		SNP		Others	
	Votes	Seats	Votes	Seats	Votes	Seats	Votes	Seats	Votes	Seats
1999										
Constituency	15.5	0	39	53	14	12	29	7	2.5	1
List	15.3	18	34	3	12.4	5	27	28	11.3	2
Total seats		18		56		17		35		3
2003										
Constituency	16.6	3	34.6	46	15.3	13	23.8	9	9.7	1
List	15.5	15	29.3	4	11.8	4	20.9	18	22.5	14
Total Seats		18		50		17		27		15
2007										
Constituency	16.6	4	32.2	37	16.2	11	32.9	21	2.1	0
List	13	13	29.2	9	11.3	5	31	26	15.5	3
Total Seats		17		46		16		47		3
2011										
Constituency	13.9	3	31.7	15	7.9	2	45.4	53	1.1	0
List	12.4	12	26.3	22	5.2	3	44	16	12.2	3
Total Seats		15		37		5		69		3

Table 1.2 UK General Election Results in Scotland 1945-2010

Year	Conservative		Labour		Lib Dem		SNP	
	Votes	Seats	Votes	Seats	Votes	Seats	Votes	Seats
1945	41.1	27	49.4	40	5	0	1.2	0
1950	44.8	32	46.2	32	6.6	2	0.4	0
1951	48.6	35	47.9	35	2.7	1	0.3	0
1955	50.1	36	46.7	34	1.9	1	0.5	0
1959	47.2	31	46.7	38	4.1	1	0.5	0
1964	40.6	24	48.7	43	7.6	4	2.4	0
1966	37.7	20	49.9	46	6.8	5	5	0
1970	38	23	44.5	44	5.5	3	11.4	1
1974 (Feb)	32.9	21	36.6	41	8	3	21.9	7
1974 (Oct)	24.7	16	36.3	41	8.3	3	30.4	11
1979	31.4	22	41.5	44	9	3	17.3	2
1983	28.4	21	35.1	41	24.5	8	11.7	2
1987	24	10	42.4	50	19.2	9	14	3
1992	25.7	11	39	49	13.1	9	21.5	3
1997	17.5	0	45.6	56	13	10	22.1	6
2001	15.58	1	43.26	55	16.37	10	20.06	5
2005	15.8	1	39.5	41	22.6	11	17.7	6
2010	16.7	1	42	41	18.9	11	19.9	6

statewide levels but its statewide representation from the region is weak to non-existent which poses questions of legitimacy for the statewide party in government [the opposite situation can be directed towards the SNP]. What did this all mean when it came to the referendum? Well, it meant that Conservative involvement in the campaign required careful management, especially at the level of the UK Government where there was a clear awareness that Conservative actions could cause problems for the No campaign. In addition, the role of the Conservatives in the Better Together coalition caused political problems for Labour and the trade unions. Not only did they not wish to associate with their historic enemies but they understood that being seen in coalition with the Conservatives would damage the party and aid the Yes campaign. The electoral damage done to the Liberal Democrats following coalition with the Conservatives in 2010 offers clear evidence of this concern. When you nest these problems within broader Westminster two-party politics and Conservative-Labour electoral competition you can understand the multi-level dimension challenges faced by Better Together.

Better Together was established in 2012 as an umbrella organization for the Conservatives, Labour and Liberal Democrats, with a titular head from Labour in the shape of former Chancellor of the Exchequer Alastair Darling, a Scottish MP [the campaign could not be run by the UK Government, Prime Minister or Conservative Party for obvious political reasons]. The organization sought to arrange local organizations and events and coordinate political communications, social media and grassroots campaigning alongside the pro-Union parties. Managing the policy and political tensions and interests between the various parties and associated organizations like the trade unions was challenging: not least because the coalition lacked ideological coherence. Two of the parties were in coalition in central government at Westminster, whilst the other was the main opposition party in Westminster and Holyrood. However, Labour was the key organization here in terms of elected representatives, activists and members, the link to the trade unions and electoral support so that the three components of the No coalition were as unequal as they were ideologically incoherent. In addition, Labour had the most to lose from Scottish independence. The Yes campaign umbrella group Yes Scotland was also a coalition between the dominant SNP and the smaller Greens, some independents and the Scottish Socialist Party. Although this coalition had more ideological coherence than the No campaign, with the SNP's moderate centre-left appeal more easily aligned with Greens, Socialists and radicals, there were some ideological and political tensions between these other parties and the SNP Government over issues like currency and the monarchy. In addition, the emergence of the Radical Independence movement offered a more radical version of the independence option than either the SNP or Yes Scotland. This development had the effect of making the Yes coalition appear broader and more diverse in one sense but also divided in another. It generated interesting debates and alternatives, not least through the Jimmy Reid Foundation think tank and development of the idea of the Common Weal, but its effect on the ground was difficult to determine.

Of course, what is important to remember about party competition in Scotland and at the referendum, is that it is not simply between Scottish and UK political actors but also involves Scottish divisions of UK political organizations and therefore a more complex multi-level electoral arena. UK political parties took steps to adapt party organization and policymaking to accommodate devolution over a number of years [Fabre and Martinez-Herrera 2009]: both in advance of devolution and even after its first decade. The existence of a territorial dimension in UK politics meant that statewide parties like the Conservatives and Labour had to accommodate territorial diversity in their policies and programmes to some extent [Van Biezen and Hopkin 2006: 15]. This influenced attitudes to devolution from the 1960s onwards and in advance of the independence referendum too, as parties reviewed their positions on further devolved powers for Scotland. The existence of a territorial dimension created tensions between different levels of party organization, some of which also increased with the onset of devolution from 1997 onwards in the UK. Within Labour, these tensions manifested themselves in relation to leader and candidate selections in Scotland, Wales and London [Bradbury 2006] and in some policy disputes between the different levels of the party in government [Hassan and Shaw 2012]. The territorial dimension created management challenges at different levels of the party.

Devolution brought organizational change to political parties in time and in different periods. For example, Labour changed its name to the Scottish Labour Party in 1994 and altered its constitutional procedures in anticipation of devolution [Lynch and Birrell 2004: 177] to choose its own leader, who was to become First Minister after the 1999 Scottish election. Scottish Labour also instituted its own version of the party-wide policymaking reforms after 1997, with the creation of a Scottish Policy Forum and a Scottish Joint Policy Committee to examine policy proposals, party strategy and the compilation of the election manifesto in Scotland [Hassan and Shaw 2012: 264]. A further set of reforms were instituted after the 2011 Scottish election though the medium of the Murphy-Boyack review of party organization, which created a more autonomous party in Scotland with a single leader and organization, though staffing, membership and finance remained matters for the statewide party [Hassan and Shaw 2012: 330]: as well as the assumption that the Scottish party was reliant upon the statewide party for financial support.

The Scottish Conservatives were not immune to organizational changes post-devolution as they struggled with the regional/national dilemma in relation to party organization, identity and electoral performance [Roller and van Houten 2003]. The party's Strathclyde Commission of 1998 sought to create a more autonomous party organization that elected its own leader, established a policy apparatus that could generate policies and a manifesto for devolved elections and also select candidates for Scottish elections independently of the UK party [Lynch 2003]. Such changes may have helped to prepare the party for devolution but did not improve its political image in Scotland or its electoral prospects. This period also saw a brief debate about whether the party should undertake more radical reorganization and set itself up independently of the UK organization [a Scottish CSU to the UK's CDU in essence] but this discussion was supplanted by official party reforms - only to return a decade later. The party's electoral failure in Scotland at the 2010 UK general election brought further organizational reforms in the shape of the Sanderson Commission report, which created a new party constitution in Scotland along with the post of party leader, elected by OMOV and responsible for the whole party in Scotland, not just the MSPs [Scottish Conservatives 2010]. The leadership contest held under these new arrangements following the 2011 Scottish election saw serious debate within the party about its identity and organization on the regional/statewide cleavage that echoed the 1997-8 period. In 2011, one leading candidate for the leadership proposed reforming the Scottish Tories as a new organization, separate from the UK similar to the situation that prevailed from 1912-1965. However, the reform candidate was narrowly defeated and the proposals for a breakaway party were shelved [Convery 2012].

Whilst Labour and the Conservatives faced challenges in addressing the regional-statewide cleavage, other parties were more fortunate. The formal federal structure of the Liberal Democrats aided the Scottish Liberal Democrat's transition to devolution as a Scottish party organization already existed, with policymaking bodies and structures. This situation insulated the party from territorial problems with the British level of the party though these came under stress following the statewide party's coalition agreement with the Conservatives following on from the UK general election of 2010. The Scottish party was a minor consideration in coalition and it was dangerously exposed at elections in Scotland in 2011 and 2012. Alongside the Liberal

Democrats, other parties faced limited organizational challenges with devolution. The Greens and Socialists operated as autonomous parties and were some of the electoral beneficiaries of the devolved electoral system though their supranational ideologies were challenged by their support for devolution and also for independence. This problem was most relevant for the Scottish Socialist Party, given the left's problems with nationalism, borders and worker's solidarity. However, a greater problem for the SSP came in the shape of the Tommy Sheridan scandal in 2006 that undermined the SSP and created a competitor party from 2007 onwards.

Experience in 1979 and 1997

The independence referendum of 2014 was Scotland's fifth 'national' referendum experience. The country experienced UK-wide referendums on membership of the European Community in 1975 and adoption of the Alternative Vote in 2011, as well as two referendums on devolution in 1979 and 1997. Besides these, there have been local referendums in Scotland on water privatization in Strathclyde [1994], congestion-charging in Edinburgh [2005], the Union Terrace Gardens project in Aberdeen [2012], as well as older referendums on alcohol licensing and one Scotland-wide privately financed referendum on retaining laws preventing teaching about homosexuality in schools [2000]. The referendums with the greatest levels of partisan involvement and of most relevance to the 2014 experience were the devolution referendums of 1979 and 1997, not least as there is some continuity in personnel between the three referendums and public memory of both previous referendums.

The two Scottish devolution referendum campaigns were notable for the partisan dimensions to each campaign. In 1979, the Yes campaign was bedeviled by partisan disputes to the extent that no coherent Yes coalition emerged in the shape of an umbrella campaign group. Indeed, there were 8 different Yes campaigns at the 1979 referendum, with little organization, fragmented messages and divided campaigning on the ground. On the surface, Yes had ideological consistency between centre-left parties, but intra-party conflict and cross-party disputes eroded this advantage. Yes for Scotland existed, having been formed on 26th January 1978, but by the time the referendum came it comprised the SNP and the dissident Scottish Labour Party, whilst the official Labour Party conducted its own Yes campaign as it did not want to 'share' the campaign and the credit with its 'separatist' opponents [see Helen Liddell's memo in Bochel, Denver and Macartney 1981: 17].

The political reality on the ground in the late 1970s was responsible for this situation, as Labour and the SNP were serious rivals in many seats across Scotland at local and Westminster levels [Canavan 2009: 199]. The result was for some Labour activists to campaign for a No vote to damage the SNP or to sit on their hands and do no campaigning but focus on the next electoral contest between the parties. Cooperation between the two parties was limited by electoral competition and political tribalism. Whilst Yes for Scotland functioned weakly, it was accompanied by individual campaigns by Labour and the SNP, as well as smaller supportive campaigns by the Conservatives, Communists and Scottish Labour Party. However, overall coordination of campaigning, strategy and political messages was lacking.

The Conservatives were a key part of the No campaign in 1979, but a careful one. The Tories were key figures in Scotland Says No, alongside members of the business community. The party had a small number of pro-devolution supporters, some in prominent positions, but was keen to manage these political differences whilst keeping its eye on the main prize – the general election in 1979, which was likely to follow the referendum [Bochel, Denver and Macartney 1981: 22-3]. Labour itself was also divided over devolution, with a substantial number of prominent Labour politicians and local activists involved in Labour Vote No. This latter development was felt in the media, in local campaigning and in the Labour movement more widely. And, Labour voters got the message. If referendums see voters using political parties as 'cues' on an issue [Zaller 1992], then the presence of an active Labour No campaign divided the effectiveness of the 'cues' coming from the official Labour Yes campaign in 1979. The activities of Labour devo-sceptics gave Scotland Says No cross-party legitimacy and there was some coordination of campaigning between the different groups.

The 1997 referendum experience was very different. Cross-party campaigning by the Yes side was effectively managed, in spite of differences between the parties. There was a degree of ideological consistency between the three main Yes parties – Labour, Liberal Democrats and SNP – as well as an awareness that parties would be key actors in the referendum campaign [Denver, Mitchell, Pattie and Bochel 1998: 52] and specifically that the campaign would need to involve the SNP to guarantee success. Hence planning and organization that began in 1996 was sensitive to the need to keep the SNP involved in Yes discussions in advance of the 1997 general election campaign at which the Nationalists would challenge Labour over devolution. The fact that the referendum was held 4 months after the general election had the consequence of detaching the contest from immediate partisan interests and all three Yes parties had political interests in the success of the referendum that would benefit them in the short and long terms. At this referendum, the Yes campaign group was called Scotland Forward and it operated as a coordinating body to produce a united Yes campaign. It was a limited umbrella body though compared to the political parties. It did undertake local campaigning and produced election materials but most of the campaign activities were conducted by the political parties. However, its efforts did maintain a cohesive Yes campaign with little political friction between the political parties so that a strong Yes coalition was maintained throughout the referendum campaign.

Ranged against Scotland Forward was the No campaign group Think Twice. Whereas Scotland Forward was planned and organized early, Think Twice was created in the summer before the September referendum. It was a one-party organization – involving the Conservatives – and this party had just experienced a shattering collapse at the 1997 general election in Scotland, when it lost all of its MPs. Think Twice failed to broaden the No coalition away from the defeated Conservatives and did not attract Labour devo-sceptics like Tam Dalyell. It did act to raise funds for the referendum, with spending of around £275,000. But it was raised late in the day and mostly spent on newspaper advertising for want of better alternatives [Denver, Mitchell, Pattie and Bochel 1998: 59], as it had very few activists on the ground able to utilize its resources.

Partisan Goals and Motives during the Long Referendum Campaign

Victory may be the stated goals of the political parties at referendums, but there may also be additional goals evident. The party may use the referendum as a mechanism to mobilize its own voters to show them it cares about an issue, defend a cause important to its supporters or seek to play an agendasetting role to gain policy concessions or reform over the issue [Bernhard 2012: 19]. A party may also use the referendum to build its organization and support base. Some may view the referendum as a distraction but it is also an opportunity to engage voters, recruit members, activate existing members and raise the party's profile and resources. Some parties find that the referendum offers them unprecedented opportunities to engage with the public and bring the party to a wider audience for the first time [Bernhard 2012: 38]: which may be relevant in the case of small parties like the Greens and SSP, as we shall see in chapter 7. Of course, partisan motives can conflict with referendum goals and parties have competitive goals at referendums that are separate from the referendum outcome. Sure enough, parties may benefit from a referendum outcome by seeking to gain political benefit or escape political blame over an issue, they may also seek to 'survive' a referendum to minimize the political downsides for the party. However, parties also have clear ulterior goals in a referendum campaign. Their campaign role and activities on the ground may link directly to the desire to hold and/or target seats at forthcoming elections, to grow support in specific geographical areas and to target certain demographic groups. Parties on the ground may therefore target their efforts quite specifically and this may be complicated by their membership of umbrella campaign groups with their main electoral competitors – and splinter local campaign efforts and cooperation. This situation was particularly prominent in the Scottish devolution referendum of 1979, as discussed above.

The Multi-level Dimension

The Scottish independence campaign cannot be examined in isolation from the UK given the manner in which the issue, political actors, voters and economic and political context were nested within a broader UK and European environment. This situation was particularly pronounced in the arena of the political parties, where three of the main parties that comprised the No campaign were divisions of British parties that needed to balance their own referendum strategy with wider political imperatives. This created very different realities for the Conservatives, Labour and Liberal Democrats during the referendum campaign. The Conservatives were the weakest actor here and susceptible to a political credibility gap given the party's 'English' identity in Scotland, its historic opposition to devolution, negative views of the UK level of the party and its electoral and organizational weaknesses in Scotland: the party had only 1 MP in Scotland 2010-15 and had faced a historic low in electoral support at the 2011 Scottish election. Conservative participation in the referendum, especially from UK-level actors like the Prime Minister, David Cameron, required careful handling. These difficulties brought some careful territorial management despite the obvious Conservative electoral interest in Scottish independence – which would remove dozens of Labour MPs from Westminster and vastly increase the prospects of majority Conservative Government.

For the Liberal Democrats, the referendum issue provided both challenges and opportunities given the party's fragile state in Scotland. The party had gained office at the UK level in May 2010 following the signing of the coalition agreement with the Conservatives. However, this development was not welcome within Scotland. The electoral consequences involved substantial losses of votes and seats at the 2011 Scottish election and the 2012 Scottish local election. Further losses of support in Liberal Democrat seats at the 2015 election were therefore a major preoccupation for the party on the ground: which sought a 'consolidation strategy' to defend sitting MPs through popularizing policy gains in office and the local record of MPs. However, the independence referendum also allowed the party the opportunity to re-establish its Scottish credentials through the conduct of its Home Rule Commission in the months after the 2011 Scottish election [Scottish Liberal Democrats 2011]. Individual Liberal Democrats were also enthusiastic participants in the Devo Plus group to increase the economic powers of the Scottish Parliament,[2] in addition to promoting the autonomy of the Northern isles of Orkney and Shetland in the context of the referendum debate.[3] Given the party's fragile organizational and electoral position in Scotland, such agendasetting might have been its major goal in the long referendum campaign.

The biggest multi-level challenge was faced by Labour as the party that created the devolved institutions and relied upon Scottish votes and seats at UK general elections to gain government office at Westminster. It had been heavily challenged by the SNP at the 2007 and 2011 Scottish elections, but performed well in Scotland at the 2010 UK election. Maintaining Scotland in the UK was central to its electoral hopes in 2015 and after – it's worth remembering that Scotland delivered 41 Labour MPs out of 258 in 2010, a sizeable contingent, especially compared to the Conservatives. Moreover, the nature of the referendum campaign dynamics also placed pressures on Labour at different levels. On the ground, party members and trade union activists were reluctant to get involved in grassroots activities with their Better Together partners, the Conservatives and Liberal Democrats: a separate group, United for Labour, was the result. In addition, efforts by the party leadership at Westminster to demonstrate economic competence by signing up to austerity budgets to compete with the coalition parties at the 2015 UK election brought difficulties for the party and its voters around the referendum issue.

Of course, the Yes side of the referendum campaign was comprised of parties with little of the multi-level constraints of the Better Together parties. The SNP, Greens and Scottish Socialist Party lacked UK-wide equivalents. This created a simpler political opportunity structure but did involve some downsides as we shall see. Sure enough, the SNP did not need to balance its referendum strategy with UK-wide considerations, but it was bedeviled by its own multi-level weakness at Westminster.

During the period of the independence referendum, the SNP remained Westminster-weak in terms of political representation, with only 6 MPs at Westminster and no members of the House of Lords. This left the party exposed at Westminster in parliamentary debates, committee investigations and media activities. Given how these influenced media coverage in Scotland in both the newspapers and television, it created a structural disadvantage for both the SNP and the Scottish Government.

Party Production of Political Discourse

One very obvious feature of party strategies generally – and during this referendum campaign – is the production of political discourse. This activity is directly related to what Lipset and Rokkan have termed the 'expressive functions' of parties, namely the construction and use of 'rhetoric for the translation of contrasts in the social and cultural structure into demands and pressure for action or inaction' [1967: 5]. In the 2014 referendum campaign, parties continued to perform this function, but at the same time carefully articulated the expression of aggregated interests as part of two broader fronts. This feature is central to our understanding of key functions of parties that have been noted earlier, and set the context within which party discursive strategies for the referendum were articulated. One of the features of the referendum campaign was the way in which it altered typical party behaviour within the party system by, temporarily, creating broad umbrella groups of parties. In this sense, in terms of the referendum campaign, party discourses serve two of the cross-cutting functions of political parties at the same time.

The first of these is as 'agents of group mobilisation' (which usually has an electoral role). The second is to build identity and solidarity of social groups with the polity and state. Party discourses serve to integrate their groups within the political system, as opposed to their other function of maximising representative strength for their own party (mobilisation). What umbrella groups are doing is splitting the integrative function into two – where there is a two way vote – and are essentially creating, *pro tempore*, something like two competing party systems. In terms of discursive strategies, the kernel of an umbrella discourse on the referendum is to mobilise consent for the political system they are promoting (which makes it slightly different from a party system in normal times). But that still means that within these respective poles, the other functions of parties are still displayed and even promoted as they compete with each other. The chapters in this volume each have sections addressing party discursive strategies in the referendum, including not just the mobilisational aspect but also the important integrative function.

In terms of the analysis of party discourses, these insights from Lipset and Rokkan regarding the expressive functions of parties within party systems help us to generate three main lines of enquiry by borrowing concepts from discourse theory:

(1) Party discourses are made up of what we could call 'essentially contested concepts' [Gallie 1964] or 'empty signifiers' [Laclau, 1996: 37], that is concepts like freedom, fairness, or democracy. These are given particular meanings in a discourse by being arranged with other concepts. So the first question we pose is what are the main concepts that a party will deploy in its discourse on a particular topic and basically how is the meaning of these concepts constructed?

(2) Parties are involved through the deployment of these concepts in 'drawing frontiers' between themselves and their opponents, what in discourse theory are referred to as 'political frontiers' [Norval, 1997: 51-76]. They try to impose their representation of the political landscape on the political debate, to articulate what the 'real' problems are, to establish who 'them and us' are, to establish important political values as opposed to false ones.

(3) The fact that parties have co-operated within umbrella groups is of interest in terms of how distinct party discourses on a range of issues can be aggregated within a wider Yes-No division between two antagonistic 'fronts'.

Discourse analysis has therefore been useful for the authors in helping to map party ideology, and identify parties' discursive strategies in terms of integration and mobilisation. While utilising a range of discourse theory concepts, the authors have focused on three particularly important categories, namely 'political frontier' [Norval 1997] 'empty signifier', [Laclau 1996: 37] and 'nodal point' [Norval 2000: 328].

Through the operation of discourse analysis based on these concepts, we can identify the principal 'empty signifiers' (understood as contested political concepts) that are used in the campaign, and which are heavily contested by the participants, concepts such as democracy, fairness, sovereignty, unity, and the like. These concepts are organised within rival discourses around what is termed in discourse theory as 'nodal points' (privileged empty signifiers that have a capacity to provide structure, purpose and a measure of overall meaning to a discourse) the most important of these being 'Independence' and 'Union', which all parties aim to construct and subvert at the same time. Therefore, the political terrain is marked out by competing 'discursive strategies'. This leads us to the concept of 'political frontier'. A political frontier is produced as a result of the political terrain being populated with more or less coherent competing discourses about the same thing that shape the terms of a political debate in such a way as to produce a political mobilisation and collective action around polarised political narratives about the past, present and future. This leads the authors in this volume to consider one further concept from discourse theory, that of 'chain of equivalence' [Laclau and Mouffe 1985]. A chain of equivalence is a feature of a political discourse that sees the arrangement of a series of empty signifiers within a chain of signification whereby they give meaning to a nodal point, in our case the nodal points are 'Union' and 'Independence'.

It is widely recognised that during recent years, political debate in Scotland and about Scotland and the UK has to a significant extent become structured according to identifiable, but shifting, positions on the constitutional question. The majority of studies to date look at the constitutional politics of Scotland and the UK from the point of view of public opinion, or other 'demand side' factors, such as socio-economic change, cultural development, or globalisation and deindustrialisation, in the search for explanations of political change. What discourse analysis offers is the opportunity to analyse how the meaning of constitutional positions has been formulated, and how dividing lines, or 'political frontiers', have been established by means of the discursive strategies of important political and societal actors, or in other words, 'supply side', focusing therefore on the nature of the messages that reach citizens and voters. It is important to bear in mind that these dividing lines have not remained fixed in time, but have evolved over the years. If discourses are the result of a process of the articulation of signifiers, the shifting boundaries between positions comes as a result of repeated re-articulation of signifiers.

It is within this context that parties, and for that matter fronts of parties – the umbrella campaign groups – deploy discursive constructs that are composed of both positive and negative chains of equivalence, making up to what they hope will become the dominant structure of ideas for the debate. How they seek to do this will be discussed for each of the parties in a section of each of the chapters.

Conclusion

Similar to many other domestic and international experiences of referendums, political parties were a key component of the Scottish independence referendum at all levels. Parties drove the issue at elections and negotiated the legislative and policy content of the referendum as governments. They were also effective producers of political discourse throughout the campaign in all areas – over policies, values, ideology, national identity, governance, etc. Similarly, the parties on the ground were central to the conduct of the referendum campaign at all levels. And, here the pattern of party engagement and activism was quite differentiated. Not only were the political parties uneven in terms of membership and resources – and this affected parties who favoured Yes as well as No – but their levels of campaign activity was quite different. For the first year of existence, the efforts of Yes Scotland and its component parties focused on soft campaigning to provide information on the referendum and independence issue. This involved existing parties but also many new activists with a less structured approach to campaigning. It sought to build new grassroots organizations using traditional techniques, plus social media. Better Together and its component parties attempted something similar but with much weaker levels of activity and engagement. However, it had a sympathetic media and the resources of the UK Government and three political parties on its side, as well as regular opinion poll leads. In any case, the role of the parties was central here and, following discussion of the international context of referendums, we will examine the role and strategy of each political party in turn.

Bibliography

Bernhard, Laurent [2012], *Campaign Strategy in Direct Democracy*, Basingstoke, Palgrave Macmillan.

Biezen, Ingrid van and Jonathan Hopkin [2006], 'Party Organization in multi-level contexts', in Dan Hough and Charlie Jeffery [Eds] [2006], *Devolution and Electoral Politics*, Manchester, Manchester University Press.

Bochel, John, David Denver and Allan Macartney [1981], *The Referendum Experience: Scotland 1979*, Aberdeen, Aberdeen University Press.

Bradbury, Jonathan [2006], ' British Political Parties and devolution: Adapting to multi-level politics in Scotland and Wales', in Dan Hough and Charlie Jeffery [Eds] [2006], *Devolution and Electoral Politics*, Manchester, Manchester University Press.

Butler, David and Austin Ranney [1994] [Eds], *Referendums Around the World: The Growing Use of Direct Democracy*, London, Macmillan.

Canavan, Dennis [2009], *Let the People Decide*, Edinburgh, Birlinn.

Convery, Alan [2012], 'The 2011 Scottish Conservative Party Leadership Contest: Dilemmas for Statewide Parties in Regional Contexts', *Parliamentary Affairs*, pp. 1–22.

Dalton, Russell and Martin Wattenberg [2002] [Eds], *Parties Without Partisans*, Oxford, Oxford University Press.

Dalton, Russell [2013], *Citizen Politics: Public Opinion and Political Parties in Advanced Industrial Democracies*, London, CQ Press.

Denver and Hands, Gordon [1997], *Modern Constituency Campaigning: Local Campaigning in the 1992 General Election*, London, Frank Cass.

Denver, David, James Mitchell, Charles Pattie and Hugh Bochel [1998], *Scotland Decides*, London, Cass.

Fabre, Elodie and Enric Martinez-Herrera [2009], 'Statewide Parties and Regional Party Competition: An Analysis of Party Manifestos in the United Kingdom', in Wilfried Swenden and Bart Maddens [Ed], *Territorial Party Politics in Western Europe*, Basingstoke, Palgrave.

Gallie, W. B, [1964], *Philosophy and the Historical Understanding*, London, Chatto & Windus.

Green, Jane [2010], 'Strategic Recovery: The Conservatives under David Cameron', in Andrew Geddes and Jonathan Tonge [Eds], *Britain Votes 2010*, Oxford, Oxford University Press,

Hassan, Gerry and Eric Shaw [2012], *The Strange Death of Labour Scotland*, Edinburgh, Edinburgh University Press.

Heath, Oliver [2010], 'The Great Divide: Voters, Parties, MPs and Expenses', in Nicholas Allen and John Bartle [Eds], *Britain at the Polls 2010*, London, Sage.

Johns, Rob, James Mitchell and Christopher Carman [2013], 'Constitution or Competence? The SNP's Re-election in 2011', *Political Studies*, Vol. 61, S1, pp. 158–178.

Johnston, Ron and Charles Pattie [2010], 'The local campaigns and the outcome', in Nicholas Allen and John Bartle [Eds], *Britain at the Polls 2010*, London, Sage.

Key, V. O. [1965], *Political Parties and Pressure Groups*, New York, Crowell.

Laclau, Ernesto [1996]. *Emancipation(s)*, London, Verso.

Laclau, Ernesto and Chantal Mouffe, [1985], *Hegemony & Socialist Strategy*, London, Verso.

Lawson, Kay [1988], 'When Linkage Fails' in Kay Lawson and Peter Merkl [Eds], *When Parties Fail*, Princeton University Press.

Lipset, S. M. and Stein Rokkan [1967], *Party systems and voter alignments: cross-national perspectives*, New York, Free Press.

Lynch, Peter [2003], 'The Scottish Conservatives, 1997-2001: from disaster to devolution and beyond', in Mark Garnett and Philip Lynch [Eds], *The Conservatives in Crisis*, Manchester, Manchester University Press.

Lynch, Peter and Steven Birrell [2004], 'The Autonomy and Organisation of Scottish Labour' in Gerry Hassan [Ed], *The Scottish Labour Party: History, Institutions and Ideas*, Edinburgh, Edinburgh University Press.

Mair, Peter [2013], *Ruling the Void: The Hollowing of Western Democracy*, London, Verso.

Mair, Peter [1994], 'Party Organizations: From Civil Society to the State', In Richard Katz and Peter Mair [Eds], *How Parties Organize: Change and Adaptation in Party Organizations in Western Democracies*, London, Sage.

Norval, Aletta [2000], 'The things we do with words - contemporary approaches to the analysis of ideology', *British Journal of Political Science*, 30, pp. 313–46.

Norval, Aletta [1997], 'Frontiers in Question', Acta Philosophica, 2, pp. 51–76.

Roller, Elise and Pieter Van Houten [2003], 'A National Party in a Regional Party System: The PSC-PSOE in Catalonia', *Regional and Federal Studies*, volume 13, no.3, pp. 1–22.

Scottish Conservatives [2010], *Building for Scotland: Strengthening the Scottish Conservatives – Report and Recommendations of the Scottish Conservatives' 2010 Commission*, Edinburgh, Scottish Conservatives.

Thorlakson, Lori [2009], 'Patterns of party integration, influence and autonomy in seven federations', *Party Politics*, volume 15, no.2, pp. 157–177.

Schneider, Gerald and Patricia Weitsman [1996], 'The Punishment Trap: Integration Referendums as Popularity Contests', *Comparative Political Studies*, vol. 28, no. 4, pp. 582–607.

Zaller, John [1992], *The Nature and Origins of Mass Opinion*, New York, Cambridge University Press.

Notes

1. In addition to this, there is limited political space on the ideological right of the left-right spectrum, evident through weak levels of support for UKIP and the BNP.
2. See the range of policy papers published by this organization at www.devoplus.org. The group was led by former Liberal Democrat MSP Jeremy Purvis and supported by former leader Tavish Scott MSP.
3. Liberal Democrat MSPs raised the issue of islands autonomy in the context of the independence debate. The islands themselves produced a joint position 'Our Islands, Our Future' which can be examined here: http://www.orkney.gov.uk/Files/Council/Consultations/Our%20Islands%20Our%20Future/Joint_Position_Statement.pdf

2

Referendums and Sovereignty

Matt Qvortrup

'As long as our world is made up of national groups which aspire to self-governance and to territorial sovereignty, ours will be a world of sovereign states and secessions from them'
                                        Pavkovic and Radan [2007:256]

Introduction

Very few countries have freely accepted that referendums on independence take place. The Soviet Union did not accept the secession of Latvia, Lithuania and Estonia through referendums. And the break-up of Yugoslavia, which was preceded by popular votes, was likewise rejected by Belgrade. True, neither Yugoslavia nor the Soviet Union were democratic states and might not be expected to be committed to the 'self-determination of the peoples'. But the opposition to the secession through referendums is not confined to authoritarian states. For example, in 1946 the Danish government did not accept the outcome of a referendum on independence for the Faroe Islands. After negotiations, the Danes accepted that the Faroese kept their MPs in Copenhagen but were granted legislative power in all areas but foreign affairs and defence. In effect the Faroe Islands got what has been called 'devolution max'. This deal was sealed when the Unionist Parties won the hastily organised general election to the Lagtinget (the Faroese legislature) shortly after the referendum [Sølvará, 2003: 156].

In this chapter the issue of sovereignty is analysed as well as when and under which conditions independence referendums have been won – and lost. First, however, a few considerations about the nature of the problem; the often complex relationship between democracy and national self-determination.

The Problem of Demos Versus Ethnos

Often in political theory deep-seated and equally axiomatic maxims often collide. Two fundamental political philosophical 'truths' are that each nation has a right to determine its own affairs and that the majority has a right to govern. Needless to say, these 'rights' are tempered by the recognition that no nation and no majority may ride roughshod over minorities. But this *caveat* notwithstanding, national self-determination and majority rule are principles which few fundamentally object to in political theory. Indeed, defending the reverse positions would appear politically absurd. But the problem is that the two principles often are incompatible. To understand why, it might be useful to consider a distinction used in ancient Greek. The Greeks make a distinction between the people as a nation (ethnos – or δϑνος) and the people as a body of citizens (demos – or δεμος)[1] In the classical city-state – or polis – the two were congruent and, in some present-day nation states, such as for example Norway or Luxembourg, the same is largely the case. But more often than not, the two concepts are in conflict. To take an example, in June 2012 the BBC reported that an otherwise undistinguished English local politician, the Conservative councillor Rob McKella, from the small town of Corby in Northamptonshire, believed that people in England should be given a right to vote on Scottish independence (this former steel town was known as 'little Scotland' because it had so many residents born in Scotland]. After all, he argued, the voters are citizens in the United Kingdom and collectively constitute the *demos*. However, most people in Scotland, by contrast, believe that only people living north of the Border should be allowed to vote as these people – perhaps alongside Scots living in the *diaspora* – constitute the *ethnos* and hence have a right to self-determination. As will be obvious, to two world-views, both based on solid arguments, do not combine. This observation is not new. Historically, referendums have often been perceived to be incompatible with nationalism. William Sumner Maine – a conservative writer from the end of the Victorian age – once mused that, 'democracies are quite paralyzed by the plea of nationality. There is no more effective way of attacking them than by admitting the right of the majority to govern, but denying that the majority so entitled is the particular majority which claims the right' [Maine 1897: 88].

This chapter should be read in the context of this tension between the *ethnos* and the *demos*, and about the problems that are raised when majority rule is employed in an attempt to resolve ethnic and national issues and problems. Our main focus is to understand the legal doctrine as opposed to the political doctrine. As we shall see, lawyers are somewhat more inflexible in these matters, and what is considered a 'right' in political theory may not always translate into a legal norm.

Referendums and Nationalism in Political History

To date there have been 49 referendums on independence. Some have been official, others unofficial. Some have been successful, and others have ended in failure. The first independence referendums were held in Texas, Tennessee and Virginia in 1861 [Qvortrup 2012]. All voted for secession, but their wishes were not granted and were resolved on the battlefield in the American Civil War. Forty-four years later Norway voted for secession from Sweden. But these votes are outliers. Generally speaking, referendums on independence have come in waves (See Figure One). Without going into a deep discussion about overall patterns it seems that momentous changes in the international system are correlated with referendums on independence. Though in this respect the Scottish referendum is something of the odd-one out!

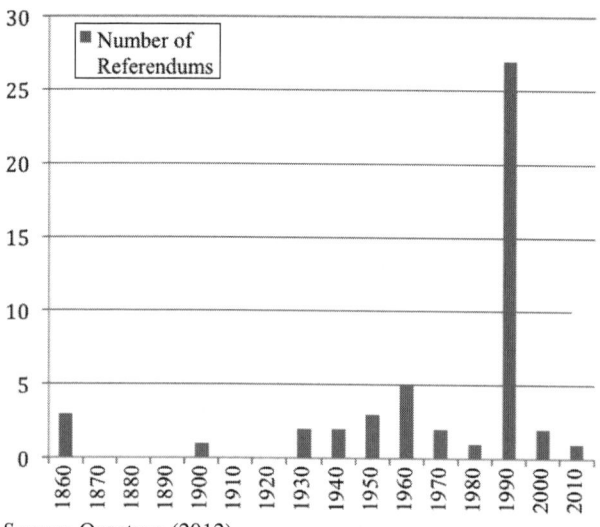

Source: Qvortrup (2012)

Fig. 1 Referendums on Independence 1861–2011

Table One: Secession Referendums 1945-2011

Country	Seceding Territory	Year	Yes vote	Turnout
Denmark	Iceland	1944	99.5	98
China	Mongolia	1945	98	64
France	Cambodia	1945	100	80
Denmark	Faroe Islands	1946	50.1	64
UK	Malta	1956	75	59
France	Guinea	1958	97	85
France	Algeria	1958	96	79
West Indian Federation	Jamaica	1961	46	60
Algeria/France	Algeria/France	1962	99.7	75.6
UK	Malta	1964	50.7	80
Canada	Quebec	1980	59	85
Yugoslavia	Slovenia	1990	94	93
USA	Palau	1990	60.8	69.2
USSR	Lithuania	1991	91	84
USSR	Estonia	1991	77	83
USSR	Latvia	1991	74	88
USSR	Georgia	1991	98	90
USSR	Ukraine	1991	70	85
USSR	USSR	1991	75.3	73
Georgia	South Ossetia	1991	98	90
Georgia	Abkhasia	1991	99	58
Yugoslavia	Croatia	1991	98	83
Croatia	Serbs	1991	98	83
Yugoslavia	Macedonia	1991	70	75
USSR	Armenia	1991	95.05	90
Bosnia	Serbs	1991	98	85
Serbia	Sandjak	1991	96	67
Serbia	Kosovo	1991	99	87
USSR	Turkmenistan	1991	94	97
USSR	Karabagh	1991	99.89	82
USSR	Uzbekistan	1991	98	94
Macedonia	Albanians	1991	99	93
Moldova	Transnistria	1991	97.7	78
Yugoslavia	Bosnia	1992	99	64
Yugoslavia	Montenegro	1992	66	96
Georgia	South Ossetia	1992	100	97
Bosnia	Krajina	1992	99	64
Ethiopia	Eritrea	1993	99	98
Bosnia	Serbs	1993	96	92

Country	Seceding Territory	Year	Yes vote	Turnout
USA	Puerto Rica	1993	48.4	73
Georgia	Abkhasia	1995	96	52
Quebec	Cris	1995	95	75
Canada	Quebec	1995	49.4	94
St Kitts and Nevis	Nevis	1998	61.8	58
Indonesia	East Timor	1999	78.5	94
New Zealand	Tokelau	2006	60.0	95
Yugoslavia	Montenegro	2006	55.5	36
Sudan	Southern Sudan	2011	98.8	98

Source: Qvortrup [2012]

In the wake of the Second World War, during the process of decolonization, several countries broke free from their erstwhile colonial overlords following successful referendums. And, in the period following the collapse of the Soviet Union there was an explosion in the number of independence referendums.

This pattern might be understandable. Countries that previously were able to prevent independence due to a combination of legal and power-political factors were unable to stem the tide of national awakening. The dynamics behind the Scottish vote – as other chapters in this book show – was rather different and should be understood within the context of a millennium of interactions between England and Scotland.

Secession in Practice

'Secession', according to Pavkovic and Radan, is a 'process of withdrawal of a territory and its population from an existing state and the creation of a new state on that territory' [Pavkovic and Radan 2007: 1].

Needless to say, secession is a process of far-reaching and irreversible consequences. Once undertaken the process of a political divorce between two groups sharing the same territory is a one-way street – and, moreover, one which often has a violent aftermath. Few countries that have split up, or from which one part has seceded, have become unified apart from Yemen. There are few political equivalents of Richard Burton and Elizabeth Taylor (who famously remarried). Yemen is the one exception to the rule. Because of the far-reaching and irreversible character of secessions it is – in an era of popular sovereignty – natural that such changes should and are expected to be ratified by the voters. John Stuart Mill – writing in *Considerations on Representative Government* – was an early and perhaps unwitting exponent of this view, when he stressed, that 'where the sentiment of nationality exists in any force, there is a *prima facie* case for uniting all the members of the nationality under the same government ... This is merely saying that the question of government ought to be decided by the governed' [Mill 1890: 234]. In other words, the people – the citizens of a particular territory – should have the final say due to the magnitude and irreversibility of the decision.

Since the American Civil War – when Texas and Tennessee voted to leave the Union – scores of referendums have been held on whether territories should secede. Sometimes these divorces have been amicable – at other times they have been acrimonious and bitter. Sometimes they have resulted in peaceful resolutions of long standing conflicts (e.g. in the case of Norway in 1905). But more often than not, these polls have resulted in exacerbated conflicts and a deepening of tensions (as was the case in Bosnia-Herzegovina and East Timor).

Generally speaking it has become an accepted norm in international relations that erstwhile colonies should be granted independence after referendums [Secretary-General, SG/SM/11568, GA/COL/3171]. This was not always the case and this change represents a break with earlier epochs, when 'the rules governing the intercourse of states [did] neither demand nor recognize the application of the plebiscite in the determination of sovereignty' [Maltern 1921:171]. This has changed, at least in the political sphere – though perhaps not, as we shall see, in the realm of constitutional law. Politically, referendums are now (once again) seen as de *rigueur* and a political *conditio sine qua non* in cases where a defined part of an existing state wishes to become independent [Beigbeder 1994:91]. UN Secretary General Ban Ki-moon has urged that erstwhile (and still existing) colonial powers 'complete the decolonization process in every one of the remaining 16 Non-Self Governing Territories' [Secretary-General, SG/SM/11568, GA/COL/3171].

The recognition that all former colonies and dependent territories should be 'free' was the formal justification for the referendums on independence in, respectively, Eritrea (1993) and East Timor (1999) – though not in the referendum in Southern Sudan in 2011. The former areas had been self-governing and were perceived to be (or were argued to be) 'colonies'. Hence, they were allowed to become independent states.[2] But things are rather different if we look at the position in constitutional law.

Independence Referendums in Constitutional Law

Historically, the question of the legality of self-determination through referendums has, as Philip Goodhart noted 'almost invariably followed national lines' [Goodhart 1971:107]. As he continued:

> For almost 25 years after the Franco-Prussian War (1870-1871) the leading French international lawyers, Montluc, Ott, Cabouat, Renan and Audinet steadily argued that the doctrine of self-determination had been established by natural right and international usage. Meanwhile the German lawyers Hotzendorf, Geffker, Stoerk and Francis Liever argued variously that plebiscites were wrong; that they subjected the minority to the rule of simple majority without protection [Goodhart 1971:111].

Before the war, the French constitutionalists had been in favour of referendums, and their German counterparts opposed to letting the people decide [Goodhart, ibid]. Expedience, it would seem, led to a change of heart. Perhaps, very little has changed. One of the most persistent and controversial questions regarding national self-determination and the referendums is who is allowed to initiate a vote on independence.

Yet for all the justified cynicism, legal issues often constrain the political logic and force actors to take decisions that may not be in their political interest. Scotland is a case in point. In 2011 the Scottish National Party (SNP) won the election to the Scottish Parliament on a manifesto commitment to hold a referendum on independence [Tierney 2012:147]. But although the SNP won a majority of the vote, the party was – as a leading constitutional lawyer noted – 'clearly aware that it would be democratically perverse, as well as politically and legally impossible, to try to override the legal legitimacy of the [Scotland] Act [1998] by way of an extra-constitutional referendum' [Tierney 2012: 147]. This situation is not so different from the situation in Catalonia where the regionalist party *Convergencia i Unió* and its allies won an election to the *Parlament de Catalunya* on a similar pledge in November 2012 [See also Guibernau 2000].

It is a key part of constitutional politics that the judiciary polices the boundaries of competencies allocated to different actors [Tarr 1997:1097]. In the context of referendums on national self-determination, this has led to several rulings regarding the constitutionality – or otherwise – of decisions by secessionist governments or sub-units decisions to hold votes on independence [Oklopcic 2012].

As a general rule, such referendums have resulted in rejections of the decisions to hold referendums on self-determination. For example, in Spain, the *El Tribunal Constitucional de España* in *Judgement No. 103/2008* held that the Basque Parliament had acted *ultra vires* and declared 'the unconstitutionality and subsequent invalidity of the *Basque Parliament Law 9/2008 of 27 June*' (a law on a referendum on *de facto* independence that followed on from Plan Ibarretxe). This ruling is similar to judgements in the United States and in Canada.

In the United States, the *Supreme Court of Alaska* ruled in 2006 that a referendum on whether Alaska could seek a legal path to independence was *ultra vires* – and could not be held [*Kohlhaas v Alaska* 147 P 3d 714, 2006]. In reaching this decision, the judges cited the earlier – and much celebrated - case of *White v Texas* from 1869, in which the Supreme Court held that a unilateral secession would be illegal under US Constitutional Law [Radan 2006: 187].

In Canada, in a much-cited case, the *Royal Supreme Court of Canada* (RSSC) held in Re Quebec in 1998 that 'any attempt to effect the secession of a province from Canada must be undertaken pursuant to the *Constitution of Canada*, or else violate the Canadian legal order' [Radan 2006: 187]. From the perspective of Canadian constitutional law, a referendum on independence would not be permitted due to the absence of a constitutional amendment [Radan 2006: 187].

Based on these cases, it is hardly surprising that opponents of Scottish independence have argued that the vote on independence in 2014 is illegal [House of Lords Select Committee on the Constitution 2012]. Needless to say, the rulings were not as unambiguous as some political practitioners would like to argue. *Re Quebec* was 'complex opinion that was far from the unequivocal statement sought by the federal government' [Tierney 2012: 143]. And in any case, the issue has now been politically by-passed by the British government, which prudently avoided a legal showdown by granting the Scottish government the right to hold a referendum through the successful negotiation of the Edinburgh Agreement in October 2012, followed by UK legislation to allow the Scottish parliament to hold a one-off referendum [Scottish Government 2012].

Self-determination after independence referendums is often thought to be a solid part of international law. As Yves Beigbeder – an international lawyer – has noted in a much cited study: 'The crucial requirement for self-determination plebiscites or referenda is the political will or consent of the countries concerned, their conviction that populations should not be treated as mere chattels and pawns in the game, but that their free vote should be the basis for territorial and sovereignty allocations' [Beigbeder 1994: 160]. In reality, matters are a bit more complicated.

It fact it is a misperception that there is a 'right' to secession under international law [Hannum 2011]. The issue is complex and we cannot do justice to the matter in a few paragraphs, but what matters is the control over the territory. To state matters briefly, under international law, a country can be regarded as independent when it is recognised by the international community. For this to happen two conditions must – as a general rule – be met. First of all, the people in the territory must express a wish to secede. (Something that was recognised by the *International Court of Justice* (ICJ) in *Case Concerning East Timor Portugal* v. Australia) and in the ICJ's *Advisory opinion on Western Sahara*. Secondly, the country must be in control of its territory. This condition is known as the *'Estrada Doctrine'*. If Scotland or Catalonia were to vote for independence and if the Scottish or Catalan governments were to be in control of the territory, then the international community would – all other things being equal - recognise these new states. But as recently hinted by Peter Radan there is no obligation to do so [Radan 2012]. Politics often supersede international law!

What Determines the Outcome of Referendums?

Once it has been determined whether a referendum can legally take place, it remains for the voters to decide. But how do they decide? Do they make their decisions on the basis of the merits of the case before them or are they inspired by other factors?

Given that most referendums were held in territories with less than impeccable democratic records (such as South Sudan, Eritrea, and East Timor) it is difficult to establish what determines the outcome of a vote on independence. But if we broaden the category to include referendums on autonomy and devolution there seems to be a tendency that voters tend to support propositions if (1) they are in favour of the proposition and (2) if the government proposing the change or the secession has been in power for a relatively short period of time. In other words, it is easier to win a referendum on devolution or independence during the honeymoon period immediately after an election – something proved perhaps by the devolution referendums in Britain in 1997. Conversely the longer you have been in office the greater the risk of losing the referendum. Why is this? One possible and credible explanation was advanced by the great American political scientist V.O. Key who in a classic analysis observed that 'to govern is to antagonize' [Key 1968: 30]. All governments break promises, fail to deliver and enact unpopular laws. The no vote in a referendum is often a positive function of the years in office, a fact perhaps most clearly shown in the Canadian referendum on a new Constitution in 1992, in which Prime Minister Brian Mulroney's personal disapproval rating after almost a decade in office was the determining factor. However, it should be noted that Milo Đukanović, the Prime Minister of Montenegro, had served as premier since 1991 when he succeeded in winning the independence referendum in 2006. The main factor behind winning an independence referendum is the voters' support for the proposition.

The big question is how this support traditionally has been won? Is it better to focus on the perceived benefits of independence? Or, is it better to appeal to the voters' heart strings? There are, as shall be shown shortly, good reasons for following former New York governor Mario M Cuomo's famous dictum that 'You campaign in poetry. You govern in prose'. This is not to say that economic arguments are not credible and powerful. Scotland certainly has a flourishing tourist industry and most of the whisky connoisseurs do prefer Scottish single malt to many other beverages. Even the argument that Scotland has generated more tax revenue than any other part of the UK can be supported by statistical evidence. But that is not how referendums are won. Referendums are won by emotions, not by economics.

It may well be the case that Scotland, to quote Alex Salmond, 'has got what it takes to be a successful independent nation'. After all, small countries such as Denmark and Finland – both with populations roughly equivalent to Scotland – have been 'successful', and have prospered even though they do not have the natural resources that Scotland is blessed with. But, the problem with this line of attack is that economic arguments rarely convince the voters in referendums.

US president Bill Clinton's campaign staff famously said 'it's the economy, stupid.' That may well be the case for general elections. Candidate elections are almost always about bread-and-butter-issues. But referendums about independence are birds of another feather and require a different tactic. The issue of independence is an emotive issue, not a rational one. In an age of globalisation, the case for independence must be based on deeper and possibly irrational passions. We have plenty of evidence for this from other countries. Of course, experiences from other nations are never repeated exactly, but recurrent patterns often occur.

A couple of examples may be useful to explain why the economic argument may prove fatal to the Yes side of the debate. In Quebec in Canada, the francophone independence party got nowhere when it used economic arguments in the first referendum held there in 1980. It lost by 20 per cent.

But in the second referendum – in 1995 – the charismatic leader of the Québécois independence movement, Lucien Bouchard, came within a whisker of securing independence when he campaigned on a theme that stressed the cultural differences between Quebec and the rest of Canada.

Similarly, when Montenegro seceded from Yugoslavia, after a referendum in 2006, prime minister Milo Đukanović did not resort to claims about the economic or even the social benefits of leaving Serbia. Rather, Đukanović made references to such matters as the historic destiny of his country, ancient battles and other issues that plucked the national, romantic heart-strings of his compatriots. He won the campaign.

Why don't economic arguments convince voters? Basically, because they are easy to refute. There are as many opinions as there are economists. But it is hard to refute emotions. 'Reason is, and ought only to be, the slave of the passions, and can never pretend to any other office than to serve and obey them', observed David Hume [Hulme, 1969 [1739]: 462] – perhaps the greatest Scotsman in history. To win the referendum in 2014, the Yes side needs to appeal to the 'passions'. Rational arguments are of secondary importance when dealing with an essentially emotive issue such as independence. So, far from questioning the tactics of the perhaps most skilled – and cunning – politician on these isles, it might be advisable for Alex Salmond and supporters of independence to follow a different approach if they are to convince a majority of the Scottish voters to vote for independence in the autumn of 2014. The SNP – and the other parties campaigning for independence – will lose if they base arguments on hypothetical economic benefits.

'In doubt, vote no', runs an old adage, which is often used by those who study referendums. You know what you have got, but you don't know what you will get. The same is often true in independence referendums. The problem with the economic arguments for independence is that, by their very nature, they are technical. And voters do not trust technical and technocratic arguments.

There are several examples of politicians who have lost by using economic arguments. In 2000, when Denmark voted on joining the euro, the then prime minister – and former economist – Poul Nyrup Rasmussen made the technical arguments for membership available to the public. Faced with hundreds of pages of econometric equations and undecipherable mathematical formulae, a large number of voters grew even more sceptical than they had been before. Needless to say, Rasmussen lost his referendum [See Qvortrup 2001]. By focusing on the economic argument, the proponents of a yes-vote unwittingly hand the initiative to the opponents who can ask the Yes side to elaborate on ever finer technical points. Such a strategy will only help those who oppose independence.

Referendums are notoriously difficult to win. As a rule of thumb, you can only win a referendum if you are ahead in the polls when the campaign starts. Those in favour of independence face an uphill struggle. But referendums have been won before from similar positions. One obvious precedent is the 1975 referendum on the EEC (the forerunner of the EU). In 1975, Harold Wilson won a massive majority in the United Kingdom's first national referendum. Just over 67 per cent voted yes to staying in the EEC (the forerunner of the European Union). But the prospects of winning seemed miniscule a year before the vote.

In June 1974, all the opinion polls suggested that the No campaign would be home and dry. And yet, a year later Wilson (and his sidekick Margaret Thatcher who campaigned vociferously for staying in the Common Market) won by a 2:1 majority. Britain's membership of the EEC was resoundingly endorsed by what had seemed an inherently Eurosceptic electorate a few months before. What did Wilson do? How did he accomplish this? The main reason was the vilification of his opponents. By painting his opponents as extremists, Wilson was able to appear as the only guarantor of stability and indeed common-sense. The opponents – above all, the arch-conservative Sir Enoch Powell and the then often vilified Tony Benn – were described as beyond the pale fanatics whose views could not be trusted. Wilson stuck to one theme the whole way through: trust me to sort this out.

Needless to say, the vote in 2014 is not a repeat of the vote in 1975, but the 1975 vote certainly provides lessons for those who want to win referendums. But winning a referendum on an emotive issue pertaining to national identity is always difficult.

Conclusion

Referendums have come in waves. Beginning in the 1860s when several of the confederate states seceded from the Union in the United States (and hence precipitated the Civil War), secessionist referendums were held in Norway (1905), the Philippines (1935) and unsuccessfully in Western Australia in 1933. Generally referendums on independence only became common after the fall of the Soviet Union, possibly because a number of Western states insisted on the ratification of declarations of independence in referendums. But referendums were also held as a kind of national celebration of the newly established unity.

Most referendums have been held in countries with relatively weak democratic institutions. The often huge yes majorities suggest that the votes are not always free and fair. But in the few independence referendums that have been held in democratic countries, it seems that governments have tended to win the plebiscites if they have taken office recently and only if there is broad popular support for independence before the campaign. Given the SNP has been in office since 2007 and that support for independence before the campaign stood at 33 percent, this is not a good omen for those supporting Scottish independence. However, these patterns are not the only determining factor. Often structural factors can be reversed by a vigorous campaign that appeals to the heartstrings rather than to the economic rationality of the voters. 'You campaign in poetry. You govern in prose', former New York governor Mario M. Cuomo's dictum is good summary of how to succeed in a referendum campaign. But winning a referendum is never easy. Before the referendum in Northern Ireland on the Good Friday Agreement, Tony Blair is reported to have received a note from an adviser who quoted the 16th century Italian political writer Nicoló Machiavelli.

The note read: 'It must be remembered that there is nothing more difficult to plan, more doubtful of success, nor more dangerous to manage than a new system. For the initiator has the enmity of all who would profit by the preservation of the old institution and merely lukewarm defenders in those who gain by the new ones, and so it is that whenever those who are enemies of a new order have a chance to attack, they do so ferociously, while others defend it half-heartedly' (Machiavelli 1994: 20).

Bibliography

Beigbeder, Y. (1994), *International Monitoring of Plebiscites, Referenda and National Elections: self-determination and transition to democracy*, Dortrecht, Martinus Nijhoff.

Goodhart, Philip (1971), *The Referendum*, London, Stacey.

Guibernau, M. (2000), 'Spain: Catalonia and the Basque Country', *Parliamentary Affairs*, 53(1), 55-68.

Hannum, H. (2011), *Autonomy, sovereignty, and self-determination: The accommodation of conflicting rights*, Philadelphia, University of Pennsylvania Press.

Hansen, Mogens Herman (1999), *The Athenian Democracy in the Age of Demosthenes: Structure, Principle and Ideology*, Norman, University of Oklahoma Press.

Hume, David (1969 [1739], *A Treatise of Human Nature*, Edited by Ernest C. Mossner, London, Penguin.

V.O. Key, Jr. (1968), *The Responsible Electorate: Rationality in Presidential Voting 1936-1960*, New York, Vintage Books.

Machiavelli, Nicoló (1994), 'The Prince' in David Wootton (Editor) *Selected Political Writings*, Indianapolis, Hackett Publishing.

Maine, H.S. (1982) [1897], *Popular Government*, Indianapolis, Liberty Fund.

Mill, J.S. (1890), *Considerations on Representative Government*, London, Holt.

Oklopcic, Z. (2012), 'Independence Referendums and Democratic Theory in Quebec and Montenegro', *Nationalism and Ethnic Politics*, 18(1), pp. 22-42.

Pavkovic A. and Radan, P. (2007), *Creating New States: Theory and Practice of Secession*, Aldershot, Ashgate.

Qvortrup, M. (2001), 'How to Lose a Referendum', in *The Political Quarterly*, Vol. 72, 2001, No.2, pp. 90-100.

Qvortrup, M. (2012), 'The History of Ethno-National Referendums 1791–2011', *Nationalism and Ethnic Politics*, 18(1), pp.129-150.

Radan, P. (2006), 'Indestructible Union ... of Indestructible States: The Supreme Court of the United States and Secession', *Legal History*, Vol. 10, 187.

Radan, P. (2012), 'Secessionist Referenda in International and Domestic Law', *Nationalism and Ethnic Politics*, 18(1), pp. 8-21.

Sølvará, H. A. (2003), 'Færøernes Statsretlige Stilling i Historisk Belysning – Mellem selvstyre og Selvbestemmelse', *Faroese Law Review*, Vol. 3, No.3, pp. 156-173.

Tarr, A.G. (1997), 'New Judicial Federalism in perspective', 72, *Notre Dame Law Review*, 1996–1997, 1097.

Tierney, S. (2012), *Constitutional Referendums: The Theory and Practice of Republican Deliberation*, Oxford, Oxford University Press.

Notes

1. In ancient Athens a 'deme' was a subdivision of Attica. Demes, as simple subdivisions of land, seem to have existed in the 6th century BC and earlier, but did not acquire political significance until the reforms of Cheisthenes in 508 BC, when enrolment in a 'deme' became a requirement for citizenship and hence voting rights. (Hansen 1999: 46)
2. By contrast, whereas 'countries' like South Ossetia, Somaliland and Northern Cyprus were not former colonies or dependent territories, hence they were not granted international recognition – despite the fact that they held referendums which were not unfair by international standards.

3

The Scottish National Party and the 2014 Independence Referendum

Kevin Adamson and Peter Lynch

Introduction

The Scottish National Party is one of the key political actors in the issue of Scottish independence. The party is the pre-eminent supporter of independence and its size and popularity eclipses other pro-independence parties by a considerable distance. Its position in government since 2007 was central to the pursuit of independence, particularly following on from its majority victory at the Scottish election of 2011. The independence referendum presented multiple challenges for the SNP though, in terms of the party in public office, central office and in the country [Mair 1994:4].

As a party in public office, the SNP had to negotiate an agreement on the referendum and produce a range of legislation and preparations to facilitate the vote.[1] It also had to produce government material and research to support its case for independence at the referendum itself. This involved government publications on regulation and competition policy [Scottish Government 2013], the transition to independence [Scottish Government 2013a] and the economic benefits of independence [Scottish Government 2013b] as well as the Scottish Government White Paper on independence in November 2013. Notably, some of the research and publications around independence were handled by specially-appointed external organizations like the Fiscal Commission Working Group [2013], the Expert Working Group on Welfare to design a post-independence welfare system for Scotland [2013] and the Expert Commission on Energy Regulation established in 2013. Besides producing policy and constitutional frameworks, the SNP and Scottish

Government were also key actors in producing political discourse around the issues of independence, the Union and the referendum. As we shall see, a variety of senior SNP figures were central to the framing of the independence question around the referendum and to the conduct of the long campaign. We shall focus on this development in a later section in this paper.

In addition, throughout the referendum campaign and beyond, the SNP had to deal with the challenge of governing Scotland in areas like education, health, local government and transport, with multiple opportunities for government and policy questions to feed into the independence issue both positively and negatively. For the party in central office, there was the task of designing a referendum campaign, working with partner organizations like Yes Scotland and political parties like the Greens and Scottish Socialist Party, and also raising funds, recruiting members, fighting elections, for the duration of the long referendum campaign. For example, the party faced Scottish Parliament by-elections in Aberdeen Donside in June 2013, Dunfermline in October 2013 and Cowdenbeath in January 2014 as well as European Parliament elections in May 2014 in advance of the referendum. In addition, it needed to maintain its preparations for the UK election of 2015 and the Scottish election of 2016: meaning raising funds and recruiting members in particular. Politically and organizationally, the SNP had a life after the referendum whether there was a Yes or a No vote. For the party on the ground, there was the challenge of working alongside political competitors in the Greens, Labour and Scottish Socialist Party to achieve a Yes vote and forming new local groups around Yes in areas where SNP local organization was as prominent as it was effective. This latter process was not without its tensions, due to the need to form new groups, networks and working methods for campaigning [particularly soft campaigning] and the different cultures of activity and organization across the different components of the Yes coalition. Moreover, given its size and level of organization, the SNP on the ground was the backbone of many local Yes groups, which created challenges for activists in terms of campaign choices and the attribution of punishment/rewards – how much should SNP activists campaign for Yes as opposed to the SNP and could these things be disentangled?

Three broad conditional factors are worth considering in relation to the SNP's strategy towards the independence referendum. First, SNP electoral success in 2007 and 2011 was built on its popularity as a policy party associated with government competence not public support for independence [Johns et al 2010]. Part of the SNP's success was achieved through separating its potential as a governing party from its constitutional preference for independence. The party's decision to support an independence referendum through the devolved parliament in its 1999 Scottish election manifesto [Scottish National Party 1999:10] provided it with two advantages. On the one hand, it signaled to voters that it was safe to vote SNP at a Scottish election without triggering immediate independence – a 'lend us your vote' strategy that significantly broadened its electorate. On the other hand, the nature of the electoral system made an independence referendum unlikely and allowed the SNP to concentrate on governing and policy delivery in office, though it did also seek to advance independence in office too. Of course, the irony here was that the party's strategy was too successful in 2011, giving it a majority at Holyrood that opened the door to the referendum, even though neither the party nor the Scottish Government were well-prepared for this eventuality,[2] and party activists on the ground had become more adept at campaigning on policy issues and competence rather than on independence itself.

Second, the onset of the referendum campaign meant that the SNP became a partner in a more complex campaign management-coordination triangle between the party organization, the Scottish Government and Yes Scotland. This triangle was made more complicated by the multi-level and ad hoc nature of local organizations. The triangle had to manage permanent local SNP, Green and SSP organizations as well as emergent local Yes groups that grew across Scotland and coordinate them through developing central community and campaigning structures in Yes Scotland. This new situation brought challenges and tensions between the various organizations and levels, which was unavoidable given the organisational imbalances between the different parties and the policy distance between moderates and radicals on the independence question. Quite different party cultures, practices and levels of experience were at play here too.

Thirdly, as Butler and Ranney explain, [1994:259] referendums can have negative effects on political parties to the extent that they can 'shatter' a political organization though internal dissension, protests by party elites, resignations and factional conflict. However, significantly, none of these aspects were evident in the SNP in the period leading up to the agreement to hold a referendum and the party had been characterized by internal consensus on goals and strategy for some time [Mitchell, Bennie and Johns 2012]. The party had post-2011 debates about referendum strategy, not least over the question type – independence alone versus a multi-option referendum – but this debate was conducted constructively with little internal conflict. Public criticism about referendum strategy came from former leading figures rather than current elites or even from the grassroots.[3] Where the party did experience divisions was over the party's decision to support Scottish membership of NATO after independence, with two MSPs leaving the party to sit as independents in the Scottish Parliament in October 2012: though each remained active Yes campaigners. Maintaining this level of internal consensus throughout a long campaign was a challenge that could be seriously undermined by a negative referendum result in September 2014. The SNP has 'ownership' of the independence issue and failure at the referendum, especially if there was a convincing victory for No could undermine the SNP at all levels. Moreover, whatever happened at the referendum, as a political party, the SNP still had to face contesting the UK general in May 2015, followed by the Scottish election of 2016: which may or may not have been the first post-independence election.

The Evolution of Party Attitudes to the Autonomy Issue

Since its formal establishment in 1934, the Scottish National Party has grappled with the political alternatives to independence. At times, this involved internal debates over the right measure of self-government, evident in early debates between its founding parties the National Party of Scotland and the Scottish Party [Finlay 1994]. At other times, there were convulsive debates within the SNP over how to respond to the devolution plans of others – most notably during the Labour government of 1974-9, with the party's MPs drawn into interminable debate over the details of devolution and referendum plans until the defeat of devolution at the referendum on 1st March 1979 [Lynch 2013, Wilson 2009]. The effects of these events cast a long shadow over the SNP [Mitchell 1996], with splits over strategy and ideology in the early 1980s as well as internal disagreement over the party's attitudes to devolution and to co-operation with supporters of devolution throughout the decade. These experiences remain highly influential today for many within the SNP who were active around the time of the first devolution referendum and remain shaped by that experience. Even after the negative experience of the 1979 referendum, the party occasionally struggled with its approach to constitutional change short of independence. The party's changing position on participation in the Scottish Constitutional Convention in 1988-9 was a case in point – as withdrawal from participation made the SNP look hostile to the types of cross-party cooperation that would lead to a Scottish parliament [Mitchell 1996]. These difficulties were only resolved after the 1997

UK general election, which saw the election of a majority Labour government able to legislate for a Scottish devolution referendum in September 1997. At this juncture, the SNP formally joined a cross-party campaign for a double Yes vote at the referendum, though it had been involved in quiet dialogue over the issue since 1996. It was able to endorse devolution in 1997, whilst making it clear it would try to improve proposals for Scottish devolution in subsequent debates in the House of Commons.

When devolution actually happened in 1999 the effect, over time, was quite dramatic for the SNP. The creation of an elected Scottish political forum plus the use of the additional member system of elections provided the SNP with a Scottish-focused institution as well as higher levels of electoral representation than ever in its history. The SNP was the main opposition party in the Scottish Parliament in 1999 and 2003, before becoming a minority government in 2007 then a majority government in 2011. This latter development also opened the door to holding the independence referendum of 2014. The advent of devolution in 1999 not only transformed the electoral and institutional status of the SNP but also, arguably, resolved some of the party's internal tensions over gradualism versus fundamentalism. Such tensions were most prominent in the 1970s and 1980s and connected directly to the devolution issue. For gradualists, devolution was a useful development that would facilitate the process of independence. Constructive engagement with devolution and with some proponents of devolution was therefore supported. For fundamentalists, independence was the goal above all and such activists were suspicious of devolution as a compromise that would undermine independence and divert the SNP away from independence. The experience of the 1974-9 period was hugely influential here as the SNP's electoral success in 1974 drove the devolution issue, which then monopolized debate within the party and ultimately failed. Five years of Westminster wrangling over devolution legislation followed by the 1979 referendum effectively chewed up the SNP and spat it out, with major internal ramifications for the party. However, the experience in 1997 was completely different. Devolution was delivered following the referendum, many leading SNP figures were elected to the new Scottish Parliament and the reality of using devolution as an institutional mechanism to achieve independence effectively lessened gradualist-fundamentalist tensions in recent decades and created a much more united party [Mitchell, Bennie and Johns 2012]. This change occurred to such an extent that 'building upon the achievements of devolution' became a central plank of SNP and Yes Scotland discourse during the referendum campaign.

Before devolution, the SNP's strategy for gaining independence involved winning a majority of Scottish seats at a UK election, negotiating independence with the UK and then putting the new constitution to a referendum in Scotland [Scottish National Party 1997]. Devolution changed this situation considerably. The devolved parliament was to be employed as a mechanism to hold a single referendum on independence, with the referendum to be held in the latter stages of a Scottish Government led by the SNP [Scottish National Party 1999]. This policy was adopted in advance of the first Scottish election in 1999 but did not become a serious prospect until after the 2007 election. Minority government enabled the SNP to embark on a consultation exercise on the constitution from 2007-9 [the National Conversation] and to publish a draft referendum bill in Spring 2010. This particular initiative was not successful but many of its attributes found its way into post-2011 referendum planning by the Scottish Government and into the Edinburgh Agreement signed with the UK Government on 15th October 2012. The majority gained at the 2011 was a surprise to the SNP, but gave the party the legislative control to form a majority government capable of passing a referendum bill as well as considerable negotiation power with the UK Government through providing a mandate for the referendum.

The SNP fought each Scottish election pledged to use the devolved structure as the platform to hold the referendum in the latter stages of the parliamentary term. The SNP's strategy here had a number of different aspects. The referendum device was a vote-gathering mechanism that would allow the SNP to separate voting for it as a policy party, as against an independence party. Voters could vote for the SNP for education, health, good government or the popularity of party leader Alex Salmond, safe in the knowledge that this vote did not mean immediate independence. Instead, the voters would know that independence could only occur through a referendum. The SNP's goal here was to demonstrate to voters that it could govern successfully and gradually build support for independence, hoping that it would translate into greater support for independence. However, whilst the SNP pursued this approach in government from 2007-11 and from 2011 onwards, it also built some support for devolution and sought to appeal to supporters of greater devolution: hence the debate over a multi-option referendum promoted by the Scottish Government in 2010 and 2012 and frequent discussion of 'more powers' for Holyrood throughout the referendum campaign.

Party Strategy for the Referendum

One of the main challenges facing the SNP post-2011 was the construction of a Yes organization and a Yes campaign. Each involved different challenges and required to be balanced with party and government activities – creating the complex organizational and strategic triangle between the Scottish Government, SNP and Yes Scotland mentioned above. This complexity involved daily coordination between the three organizations, movement of staff between them and efforts to ensure consistency of message. Organisation also involved a central paradox for the SNP. The SNP was central to Yes in all sorts of ways but could not be seen to dominate Yes – it therefore had to seek to practice 'differentiation' from Yes and allow Yes a life of its own and the opportunity to implement an organizational strategy that was unfamiliar to many in the SNP (and subject to criticism at the grassroots). Running a new, community-based campaign for a two-year time period was a challenge to party activists and organization. Timing and sequencing of campaigning became important during the long campaign. In addition, despite being Scotland's leading party with a popular leader and government, the SNP needed to tread carefully in relation to Yes, in the knowledge that many people who may vote Yes disliked the SNP and its leader Alex Salmond. Similarly, one of the key tactics of the No campaign and its associated parties was to completely identify Yes with the SNP and with Alex Salmond. As the SNP effectively 'own' independence and Alex Salmond was both popular and unpopular amongst some voters this tactic was not surprising. No campaigners liked to frame independence as 'a constitutional obsession' and make references to 'Alex Salmond's referendum' to reinforce a negative link between the referendum and the SNP and ignore the existence of a wider non-SNP Yes community.

As discussed above, the SNP's role in the independence referendum involved a fundamental paradox, involving strengths and weaknesses. On the one hand, the SNP was obviously central to the Yes campaign in almost every conceivable way. The SNP's electoral success had driven the independence issue and was the reason for the referendum. The party was the largest component of the Yes Scotland campaign in terms of participation and funding but there were attempts to mitigate this position. For example, Yes Scotland was not run by the SNP but was co-managed by independents, Greens, Nationalists and Socialists in terms of its advisory board and staff. Its chair was non-party Dennis Canavan, formerly of Labour and its chief executive was Blair Jenkins, who had never joined a political party. Yes Scotland was styled as a cross-party and non-party community campaign and sought to recruit supporters and funders on that basis. Many of its activists may well have been party members, but the vast bulk of its 400,000+ registered supporters in 2013 obviously weren't. Yes Scotland's activities involved a mix of cross-party and non-party people in relation to public meetings, media events and TV appearances. This deliberately provided a strong role to non-party figures and the Greens in particular, who played prominent roles in Yes Scotland. Despite this, funding and local organization was strongly SNP-oriented at least in its initial period. The campaigning style of Yes was also quite distinctive to that of the SNP and unfamiliar to the party's activists. Yes Scotland concentrated on 'soft' campaigning through adopting a bottom-up strategy to construct community organizations through information stalls, public meetings, ambassador training and extensive use of social media. In time, Yes did adopt more traditional election-type techniques like doorstep canvassing, with results fed into the organisation's voter database (YesMo) from September 2013 onwards. However, in the first year of campaigning, its efforts were focused on creating community organizations and introducing a range of themes and topics into the referendum debate to build support and take undecided voters along the journey to supporting Yes by the time of the referendum.[4] And, with a more fluid, less-structured and hierarchical grassroots organization than a party, the campaign on the ground was active and positive.

In terms of organization and resources, the SNP was central to many local Yes groups because its campaign infrastructure far outweighed that of the Greens and Scottish Socialists. The SNP had branches and Constituency Associations across Scotland and ran a sophisticated electoral machine, with an effective voter database, telephone and door canvassing operation. By contrast, the Greens had 15 local parties organized within the 8 regional lists areas for Scottish elections and the SSP had a range of local organizations in the main cities like Dundee, Edinburgh and Glasgow. SNP membership rose to 25,000 in March 2013, whereas the Greens recorded only 1,271 at 31st December 2012,[5] and the Scottish Socialist Party reported around 600 members, although the independence referendum combined with issues like the bedroom tax gave the party a new lease of life. All three parties also had members involved in the Radical Independence campaign group too, which also emerged to undertake local campaigning activities during the referendum campaign (see chapter 7). In addition, the referendum campaign saw the launch of Labour for Independence, a campaign group of Labour members and supporters in favour of Scottish independence.[6] It was active nationally and locally during the campaign but its membership and influence was difficult to determinate. Its political relevance lay in the fact that a number of Labour voters favoured independence as well as increased devolution and clearly saw independence as a mechanism to completely escape from Conservative government. The large Labour and SNP electorates concerned with fairness and social justice were key battlegrounds in the referendum campaign and Labour for Independence played a role here as well as providing further ideological coherence to the left of centre Yes coalition.

The institutional differences between the political parties involved in the Yes campaign were very clear. The SNP had 65 MSPs, 6 MPs and 2 MEPs, compared to just 2 Green MSPs and no SSP MSPs. In terms of councillors, the SNP had 424 councillors, compared to 14 Greens and 1 SSP councillor. In terms of finance, there were huge disparities between the different parties too, with the SNP sitting as the best-funded party in Scotland with £5,030,916 income in 2011 and a further £2,300,459 in 2012. Whilst some of this income came from large donors – not least the Euromillions lottery winners and the late poet Edwin Morgan – the party also generated substantial regular income from membership fees, party conferences and fundraising. Its members were also regular donors to the party centrally and locally. The membership fees alone generated £550,205 in 2012, before adding in donations, income from party conference etc. The incomes of the Greens and SSP were dwarfed by these figures. For example, at the end of 2012, the Greens reported total income of £100,083,[7] whilst the SSP reported total income of £36,032.[8] On the face of things this still meant that the broader Yes campaign was strongly-resourced, though how much these resources were devoted to the referendum and how much party members and supporters of the Yes coalition contributed to Yes Scotland itself was difficult to determine.

The level of campaigning resources between the various Yes actors was heavily weighted to the SNP and this fed into the initial financing of Yes Scotland. The first public release of information on donations in April 2013 revealed that £1,283,000 came from five large donors, all associated with the SNP in one way or another, compared to £112,000 from over 7000 small donors. In addition, there was a £342,797 non-cash donation from the SNP to Yes Scotland's start-up costs. Yes Scotland aimed to become self-financing through donations both small and large during the campaign. In addition, many of the larger donors to recent political campaigns had yet to donate by time of writing, though they may donate to the SNP or to Yes Scotland or both before the end of the regulated donations period in May 2014. To these official figures for Yes Scotland, there were donations and activities by the SNP, Greens and SSP centrally and locally, along with organizations like Radical Independence, National Collective and Labour for Independence, so that there were additional resources for the Yes campaign in relation to cash and non-cash items that were not part of the official Yes Scotland organization.[9] Determining the level of finance here was impossible though. At some stage, these donations would start to count under Electoral Commission rules following the Edinburgh Agreement of October 2012. However, these rules did not apply until 29th May 2014 as it was only the last 16 weeks of the campaign that were regulated by the Electoral Commission. At this stage, the Commission limits meant that Yes Scotland and Better Together could spend up to £1,500,000 each. In addition, using the Scottish election of 2011 as a benchmark, the Commission allocated spending of £1,344,000 to the SNP, £834,000 to Labour, £396,000 to the Conservatives, £201,000 to the Liberal Democrats and £150,000 to the Greens [Electoral Commission 2013:1]. These regulated spending arrangements involved a combined total of £2,994,000 for Yes compared to £2,931,000 for the No campaign in the last phase of the referendum campaign. The sums involved were likely to be spent on advertising, media, campaign tours and election literature in the final weeks of the referendum campaign.

After 2011, the SNP faced two major challenges in government. First, there was the challenge of organizing the independence referendum. This was not merely a legislative task but a highly political one involving negotiations with the UK Government and the role of the Electoral Commission. The Scottish Government needed to clarify its post-2011 position on the referendum, announce its intentions, run a large consultation process, undertake negotiations with the UK Government [that overlapped with negotiations over the Scotland bill] leading to the Edinburgh Agreement and then begin to prepare for the White Paper on Independence and to produce the legislation to implement the referendum and the franchise extension. At the time of writing, the SNP was in the middle of these latter stages, with referendum legislation proceeding through the Scottish Parliament and different aspects of the Scottish Government's independence offering becoming public in the lead up to the White Paper in November 2013. Furthermore, during the first year of this process, the Scottish Government and SNP had to deal with the issue of the second question, and the prospect of a multi-option referendum. This particular concern required careful handling at all levels, within the SNP itself and also across Scottish society, with a range of groups and organizations interested in this issue.

Second, there was the more general issue of governing - meaning continuing the job of governing Scotland whilst engaged in the referendum issue. This was problematic in two ways. On the one hand, there was the obvious problem of any contemporary issue reflecting on the independence question in a negative way. Any policy difficulty or administrative problem could have negative consequences for the constitutional issue. For example, how would the SNP's support for same-sex marriage affect support for independence? Would problems in the hospital sector undermine public confidence in the SNP's competence as a government and dent its popularity, with a knock-on effect on independence? Even questions more directly connected with the constitutional issue – such as whether the SNP government had sought legal advice on Scottish membership of the EU under independence, became problematic. In addition, there was what the SNP's opponents called the 'distraction' question. Opponents in the Scottish Parliament would routinely link policy or governance problems to the SNP's 'constitutional obsession' with independence claiming that Ministers had their eye off of the ball because of dealing with the referendum and that Scotland was 'on pause' until after the referendum.

Of course, if the SNP were not in government with a majority, there would have been no referendum at all. However, government status did bring risks in relation to the referendum – risks evident at the 1979 Scottish devolution referendum – referred to as the 'punishment trap' problem. Here, the voters may use the referendum to demonstrate their dissatisfaction with the government of the day and use the referendum as a device to do so, rather than vote on the merits of the proposal on the ballot paper itself [Schneider and Weitsman 1996]. Moreover, voters do so in the knowledge that they may well return to support the party come the general election for the elected institution involved. In some senses this is a logical response to the SNP's own strategy of using the referendum device to show voters that it was 'safe' to vote for the party at a Scottish election in the knowledge that voter support meant a referendum not immediate independence.

Partisan Motives, Goals and Behaviour During the Long Referendum Campaign

One interpretation of the referendum issue was to view the SNP as the party with most to gain and most to lose out of the process, depending on the result. With a Yes vote, the SNP would clearly win through achieving its fundamental political goal and then capitalizing on this situation at the 2015 and 2016 elections. Referendum success could entrench the SNP as Scotland's governing party for some time to come. Defeat at the referendum could have the reverse effect, in undermining and demoralizing the party in advance of the UK and Scottish elections so that it entered a spiral of decline. Of course, there are important caveats here. Was a Yes loss a hefty defeat or a marginal loss? If Yes was above 40 per cent, then this would be a big electorate for independence. Similarly, short-term defeat for the SNP in 2014 would not be the end of the story for the party as Quebec's two referendums – and prospect of a third – demonstrated. However, whatever scenario came to pass at the referendum and in its aftermath, the SNP was playing for very high stakes, not least for a party that excelled at the Scottish election of 2011 and wanted to maintain and build upon that level of support in future elections.

Like its competitors, the SNP can be seen to have a range of partisan motives during the referendum that were ulterior to the referendum itself. Organizational growth is one particular aspect. The SNP experienced considerable organizational growth since the Swinney organizational reforms of the party in 2004 [Lynch 2013]. These reforms created a centralized membership scheme and enfranchised party members through the use of OMOV for electing the party leadership and for candidate selection. These reforms, coupled with increased electoral-professionalism [Panebianco 1988], saw the party increase membership, financial resources and electoral support year on year leading up to the 2011 Scottish election and beyond. This process reversed prevalent trends across political parties in the UK and in other advanced industrial democracies [Dalton 2013] as SNP membership grew markedly and moreover, these members demonstrated higher than average levels of political activism [Mitchell, Bennie and Johns 2012]. SNP membership was only 9,450 in 2003. However, this increased to 13,994 by the end of 2007 and then up to 24,732 at the end of 2012. Finances were also strong as indicated above. Organisational growth preceded electoral growth and this process continued into the referendum campaign period. The challenge for the SNP was to continue along this growth trajectory at the same time as helping to create Yes Scotland. The Yes umbrella required staff, financial resources and footsoldiers – a lot of which would come from the SNP. If SNP supporters donated to Yes Scotland would they continue to donate to the party? If party activists turned their attention to Yes stalls, leafleting and canvassing, where did this leave the SNP and its attempts to build on the successes of 2011?

For example, in 2011, the SNP won a record number of first past the post seats in Scotland. The question for the party was how to capitalize on this development to maintain and/or increase support in these new areas to feed through to the UK general election of 2015 and then the Scottish election of 2016? Personnel and resources devoted to Yes activities were consistent with SNP goals but not completely aligned and it's easy to see a level of competition and choice here for the SNP on the ground over how much to devote to the party versus the referendum campaign and whether this was seen as consistent or inconsistent? On the ground, the SNP was the most active in building Yes organizations. This development would likely accrue benefits to the SNP in terms of increased membership and support and also increase its campaigning profile in new areas, but it still involved a diversion of resources and effort: the unintended consequences of the referendum campaign. The plus side of this problem was that the only scheduled national elections were the European elections in May 2014 – not a high profile and labour-intensive electoral contest like the Scottish or UK elections. In any case, though the party's independence option trailed in opinion polls, the party itself remained a popular government and option for voters. For example, the Panelbase opinion poll for the Sunday Times/ Real Radio on 28th July 2013 found the SNP supported by 48 per cent on both the constituency and list votes, with its nearest competitor Labour on 30 per cent and 25 per cent. This poll came after the party had experienced months of sustained attacks over its leadership [with highly personal attacks on Alex Salmond], its record in government and its policy of independence.

If there were a Yes vote, the SNP would face a range of immediate challenges. Scottish Government activities would be dominated by post-referendum negotiations with the UK government and European Union as well as the policy and institutional preparations in the transition to independence. Meanwhile, the SNP's organisation and membership would face a series of electoral contests such as the UK general election of May 2015. Whether the SNP could improve on its weak performance at UK elections in 2015 was open to question. At this contest, the SNP would seek to capitalize on referendum success to gain seats from Labour and the Liberal Democrats to bolster its negotiating position in post-referendum negotiations with the UK government. The SNP would aim to win seats from the Liberal Democrats in the manner in which it did in 2011, though Labour has similar aims and shared some of its target seats with the SNP. If there were a No vote, the question is what happens to the SNP organization and electorate? SNP performance at UK general elections has been relatively poor in the post-devolution period. At these elections, the party struggled to campaign effectively and win seats outside of its heartland areas. Would a No vote depress this performance even further, with activists demotivated and exhausted after the referendum defeat and leave the party vulnerable to seat losses at the Westminster election? That is certainly what Labour was counting on in the hope that it could retake seats such as Dundee East and Western Isles whilst being the beneficiary of widespread defections from the Liberal Democrat electorate.

The SNP's Discursive Strategy Towards the Referendum

One of the most striking things in reviewing the SNP's discursive strategies since 1999, particularly on the central questions regarding sovereignty, the role and status of the parliament, and the prospects offered by independence, is continuity. This is evident in the consistency of the discursive strategies adopted by the party in the face of changing circumstances, both at the Scottish level, and at the UK level. The intention of the SNP to promote itself as a potential party of government within the remit of the devolved institutions is stated alongside the party's policy in favour of a referendum on independence, thus portraying the party as one with a dual purpose, contrary to its detractors who generally characterise the SNP as being 'obsessed' with independence.[10] At the very least, from the vantage point of 2013, this strategy has clearly borne fruit.

Of the numerous discursive strategies that the SNP adopted in 1999 for the inaugural Scottish elections, the following four enduring core strategies can be identified:

(1) to continue to reinforce the principle of the 'sovereignty of the Scottish People'
(2) to articulate Holyrood as the most important and democratically legitimate political institution in Scotland
(3) to establish the SNP as a credible party of government with interests in the governance of Scotland under the devolved settlement until such time as a referendum victory for independence could be secured and thereafter
(4) To establish the legitimacy of the principle that Scotland, through this parliament, has a right to hold a referendum on matters pertaining to the UK constitution [Scottish National Party 1999].

In terms of reaching a new stage in the deployment of its discursive strategies, the narrow election victory of the SNP in 2007 created an entirely novel platform for the SNP. The SNP continued with its four core strategies, but now, as a governing party, it was in a position to concentrate on building its credibility as a party in government and articulating its policy programme. This was presented as tailored to Scotland's specific values and requirements whilst always regretting that more could not be achieved due to the limits of devolution. From 2007-11, several elements stand out as important to the evolution of the SNP's discursive strategies. Firstly, the SNP Government democratized its independence discourse by offering their plans to the public to comment upon – the National Conversation. Launched in August 2007, this strategy fed the sovereignty strand of the discourse and enabled the scope of the Independence discussion to widen from an issue of party competition to all citizens. This strategy was successful in maintaining the prominence of the referendum as a central subject of political debate. At the same time, the SNP claimed to be effectively maximizing the possibilities of devolution as a 'responsible government' but within the 'constraints' of the Scotland Act 1998, a discourse that was encapsulated by the political frontier established by the title of the 2011 manifesto 'Re-elect a Scottish Government working for Scotland'. The period was characterized by the positive articulation of 'devolution' and 'independence' as points along Scotland's journey thus: 'Scotland is on a journey and the path ahead is a bright one' [Scottish National Party 2011:1].

In preparation for the May 2011 election the SNP relentlessly articulated two main ideas to support their claim on the necessity of a referendum on independence. Firstly, to advance a picture of the SNP as a competent government standing up for 'Scottish interests' as part of a chain of equivalence on the positive side of the political frontier including 'SNP', 'Scottish people', 'Scotland first', 'referendum', 'democracy', 'good governance' 'more powers', together with the nodal point of 'Independence'. For example, 'Scotland is on a journey. This manifesto....sets out our ideas and ambitions for the next five years. With an SNP Government putting Scotland first, there is much more we can achieve' [Scottish National Party, 2011:2] and 'We think the people of Scotland should decide our nation's future in a democratic referendum' [Scottish National Party, 2011:28]. Secondly, the SNP discourse characterized with numerous examples the nature of Westminster as an obstacle to the advancement of Scottish interests, despite the best efforts of the SNP government. This forms the basis of the negative chain of equivalence, associating 'Westminster' with 'obstacles', 'constraints', 'London parties' and the nodal point 'Union'. For example, 'The SNP in government has acted to identify savings... to allow us, as far as possible, to protect public services... We are faced with unprecedented Westminster budget cuts as a result of the reduction in Scotland's block grant' [Scottish National Party, 2011:8].

In the manifesto and during the election campaign, the SNP adopted three positions for which it sought endorsement, effectively rendering the constitutional status of the referendum as important an election issue as the actual topic of the referendum. Firstly, the party re-affirmed its commitment to legislate for a referendum in the new parliament [Scottish National Party, 2011:28]. Secondly, SNP leaders continued to remain open-minded about a further devolution option on the ballot paper, alluding to this in the manifesto which set out the aim to 'bring forward our proposals to give Scots a vote on full economic powers through an independence referendum' [Scottish National Party, 2011:3]. Thirdly, during the election campaign, Alex Salmond publicly committed to a referendum in the 'second half of the parliament'.[11]

In terms of discursive opportunity structures [Koopmans and Statham, 1999:228] the result of the 2011 general election marked a watershed moment for the party that was now in a position to claim that the Scottish electorate had endorsed the three principles outlined above. The discursive terrain upon which the SNP operated was therefore transformed. The election result was also used by the SNP to claim that the Scottish people valued 'good governance', returning the SNP for a second term in office with an increased majority [Scottish Government, 2011a]. Moreover, 'good governance' continued to be articulated together in a positive chain of equivalence with 'democracy' and 'independence'.

These three positions, along with the parliamentary majority, helped to legitimize the position that the SNP had taken on the relationship between the 'People of Scotland', the 2011 election, the Scottish Parliament, the referendum, and independence. This was an important element in the party's discourse in the period leading up to the *Edinburgh Agreement* [Scottish Government 2012]. It is reflected in the agreed text, as well as the articulations of the party about the legitimacy and legal status of the referendum during the negotiations with Westminster. Moreover, the *Edinburgh Agreement* itself was quickly articulated by the SNP in line with its core principles, becoming in itself an object of SNP constitution-building discourse.[12] Alex Salmond set out his view to members of the SNP thus:

> The Edinburgh Agreement ensures that, not only is the referendum made in Scotland, but that whatever the decision taken by the people of Scotland, it will be respected by all.[13]

Although the Yes campaign was established months before the Edinburgh Agreement was signed, the agreement paved the way for the referendum campaign to begin in earnest. The first discursive strategy of the SNP in preparing the Yes campaign was to make a distinction between the SNP as a party and Yes Scotland as a 'community-based campaign'.[14] This produced a different structure for discursive production from that adopted by the party and the government for the campaign to hold a referendum. The new strategy was officially launched in May 2012, and the intention of the SNP to relinquish outright control of discursive production was stated and demonstrated at the outset with the presence at the launch of a variety of prominent non-SNP figures lending their support to the campaign, including co-leaders of the Scottish Greens and the Scottish Socialist Party.

The most important part of the SNP's discourse now shifted back to arguments about why independence is necessary. The independence chain of equivalence constructed by supporters of Yes Scotland that articulates the positive attributes associated with independence includes the following empty signifiers (although this list is by no means exhaustive it contains some of the signifiers most frequently associated with 'independence': 'Scotland', 'fairness'; 'democracy', 'sovereignty', 'parliament', 'wealth', 'resources' 'the people of Scotland', 'potential', 'vision', 'healthy', 'natural', 'economic development', 'stable economy', 'better', 'nation' and 'strong public services'. For example, this was articulated in a speech by Nicola Sturgeon in 2012, and forms the rhetorical structure for the SNP's approach to why independence is necessary. Her vision of independence involves 'Bringing the powers home to build a better nation' in order to forge:

> A country with a stable economy that works for the many and not just the few; one that knows it must create the wealth it needs to support the strong public services we value; a country that manages our vast resources responsibly, with an eye to the future; a country that gets the government it votes for; a country that has fairness at its core and allows all of us as individuals to reach our full potential.[15]

Therefore, 'independence' functions as the nodal point that is supported by the articulation of other signifiers around it in the positive chain of equivalence. More often than not this is juxtaposed with the negative chain of equivalence around the nodal point of 'Union' or 'Westminster rule'. For example, from an SNP press release in response to comments from Secretary of State for Scotland MP Michael Moore, these signifiers and chains of equivalence structure the response:

> ....just one of the ways people and families will gain from independence is because we won't have Tory-led governments at Westminster imposing disastrous policies on Scotland against our will. These include the Bedroom Tax – which 90 per cent of Scottish MPs voted against – and George Osborne's failed austerity agenda, with a slashing of infrastructure spending. A Yes vote for independence means completing Scotland's home rule journey, so that we have the political and economic powers in Scotland to

take the decisions that are right for Scotland. Leaving decisions in the hands of Westminster is what is causing real upheaval to tens of thousands of families and vulnerable people in Scotland right now, though unfair measures such as benefits cuts for hardworking families, while the tax for millionaires is cut.[16]

As recently as August 2013, the SNP continued to contrast Westminster unfavourably with the Scottish Government in re-iterating the location of the political frontier at the heart of their referendum discourse:

> The fact of the matter is that the Westminster system is failing to serve the interests of people living here. With a Yes vote in next year's referendum, we will gain the opportunity to make decisions that always reflect the priorities of people in Scotland – rather than those of Westminster.[17]

Party Strategy and Multi-Level Politics

Whilst the SNP became the majority party at the Scottish election in 2011, it remained politically weak in multi-level terms. Whilst it could boast a large number of MSPs and councillors in Scotland, its representation at Westminster and in the European Parliament was much more limited. And, this reality left it politically exposed over the independence issue in political institutions outside of Scotland – and that's before thinking about UK Government representation in international organizations and its diplomatic presence. The SNP did not need to work through the multi-level political challenges faced by its opponents in relation to the referendum but its Westminster-weakness allowed its opponents to challenge its positions in fundamental ways. For example, the SNP's opponents in the House of Commons and Lords were able to combine to attack the referendum and independence in parliamentary debates, question time sessions and committee inquiries. When it came to parliamentary committees, the SNP was represented on the Scottish Affairs Committee but its representative stopped attending the committee following allegations of bullying by the committee chair. The outcome of this was that a variety of UK parliamentary committees could frame and conduct inquiries without SNP involvement. The Scottish Affairs Committee published a number of reports as part of its inquiry into the 'Referendum on Separation for Scotland'. The Select Committee on Defence conducted an inquiry into the 'Defence Implications of Possible Scottish Independence'. The Foreign Affairs Committee held an inquiry into 'The Foreign Policy implications of and for a Separate Scotland'. In the House of Lords, the Economic Affairs Committee conducted an inquiry into 'Scottish independence'. All of these inquiries were an opportunity for opponents to marshall evidence to attack the Scottish Government's independence proposal on an ongoing basis, providing critical material for the Better Together parties and campaign group and for the media that reported the various evidence sessions and reports and cited critical evidence and recommendations against independence. There was little the SNP could do at Westminster to deal with this, though the Scottish Parliament began to hold its own inquiries into major independence issues into 2014, which would even up its institutional weakness and generate more positive media headlines.

Conclusion

The Scottish National Party's centrality to the independence referendum is indisputable and involved both pluses and minuses. As the biggest political actor in Yes Scotland by some distance and the majority government, it had the potential to dominate the political debate and make the Yes campaign appear lopsided: something its pro-Union opponents were keen to exploit. However, the SNP's prominent position also brought clear benefits for Yes in terms of experience, strategy, finance and activists with many SNP members forming the backbone of Yes groups up and down the country. The party's role in government also provided it with the mechanism to hold the referendum in the first place, determine its format and rules in conjunction with the UK Government and Electoral Commission and also shape the content of independence through publications like the White Paper *Scotland's Future* [Scottish Government 2013c] and the work of institutions like the Fiscal Commission Working Group. Finally, the SNP was active in defining and contesting the nature of independence and the Union through its use of political discourse, a discourse that goes back to the start of devolution after the UK general election of 1997. Whether these plus points and discursive strategies are sufficient to achieve a Yes vote in 2014 is an open question though, either way, the SNP will survive as a political actor after the referendum.

Bibliography

Butler, David and Austin Ranney [1994] [Eds], *Referendums Around the World: The Growing Use of Direct Democracy*, London, Macmillan.

Dalton, Russell [2013], *Citizen Politics: Public Opinion and Political Parties in Advanced Industrial Democracies*, London, CQ Press.

Electoral Commission [2013], *Electoral Commission advice on spending limits for the referendum on independence for Scotland*, Electoral Commission.

Expert Working Group on Welfare [2013], *Expert Working Group on Welfare Report*, Edinburgh, Scottish Government.

Finlay, Richard [1994], *Independent and Free: Scottish Politics and the Origins of the SNP*, Edinburgh, John Donald Publishers.

Fiscal Commission Working Group [2013], *First Report – Macroeconomic Framework*, Edinburgh, Scottish Government.

Johns, Rob, David Denver, James Mitchell and Charles Pattie [2010], *Voting for a Scottish Government*, Manchester, Manchester University Press.

Koopmans, R. and P. Statham (1999), 'Ethnic and Civic Conceptions of Nationhood and the Differential Success of the Extreme Right in Germany and Italy', in Giugni, M., McAdam, D., and Tilly, C. (Eds), *How Social Movements Matter*, Minneapolis/London, University of Minnesota Press.

Lynch, Peter [2013], *SNP: The History of the Scottish National Party*, Cardiff, Welsh Academic Press.

Mair, Peter [1994], 'Party Organizations: From Civil Society to the State', In Richard Katz and Peter Mair [Eds], *How Parties Organize: Change and Adaptation in Party Organizations in Western Democracies*, London, Sage.

Mitchell, James, Lynn Bennie and Rob Johns [2012], *The Scottish National Party: Transition to Power*, Oxford, Oxford University Press.

Mitchell, James [1996], *Strategies for Self-Government*, Edinburgh, Polygon.

Panebianco, A. [1988], *Political Parties: Organization and Power*, Cambridge, Cambridge University Press.

Schneider, Gerald and Patricia Weitsman [1996], 'The Punishment Trap: Integration Referendums as Popularity Contests', *Comparative Political Studies*, vol. 28, no. 4, pp. 582-607.

Scottish Government [2013], *Economic and Competition Regulation in an Independent Scotland*, Edinburgh, Scottish Government.

Scottish Government [2013a], *Scotland's Future: from the Referendum to Independence and a Written Constitution*, Edinburgh, Scottish Government.

Scottish Government [2013b], *Scotland's economy: The Case for Independence*, Edinburgh, Scottish Government.

Scottish Government [2013c], *Scotland's Future*, Edinburgh, Scottish Government.

Scottish Government [2012], *Agreement between the United Kingdom Government and the Scottish Government on a referendum on independence for Scotland,* at http://www.scotland.gov.uk/About/Government/concordats/Referendum-on-independence

Scottish Government [2011], *Programme for Government 2011-12*: First Minister's statement to Parliament, (2011) http://www.scotland.gov.uk/News/Speeches/ProgrammeforGov-2011-12

Scottish National Party [2011], *Manifesto 2011: Re-elect a Scottish Government working for Scotland*, Edinburgh, Scottish National Party.

Scottish National Party [1999], *Scotland's Party, Scotland's Parliament: Manifesto for the 1999 Elections*, Edinburgh, Scottish National Party.

Select Committee on Economic Affairs [2013], 'Second Report Economic Implications for the United Kingdom of Scottish Independence', London, House of Lords.

Select Committee on Foreign Affairs [2013], 'Sixth Report - Foreign policy considerations for the UK and Scotland in the event of Scotland becoming an independent country', London, House of Commons.

Wilson, Gordon [2009], *SNP: The Turbulent Years 1960-1990*, Stirling, The Scots Independent.

Notes

1. See *Scottish Independence Referendum [Franchise] bill,* introduced on 11th March 2013 and *Scottish Independence Referendum bill,* 21st March 2013.
2. On the other hand, the Scottish Government had conducted a 3-year consultation on the constitution from 2007-9 and published a draft referendum bill in 2010 that fed into the Edinburgh Agreement 2012.
3. See for example http://www.optionsforscotland.com/ or the work of pro-independence economists here: http://www.cuthbert1.pwp.blueyonder.co.uk/
4. In some ways, Yes activity in the initial year or so contrasted with a more electorally-focused SNP's election campaign which concentrated on identifying support and feeding it into the Activate database. However, some of this campaigning style was a result of the need to tailor activity to the long referendum campaign itself as opposed to a five week election campaign. It took some time for SNP activists to grasp this difference.
5. Scottish Green Party, statement of accounts for year ended 31st December 2012, p.3.
6. See www.labourforindy.com.
7. Scottish Green Party, statement of accounts for year ended 31st December 2012.
8. Scottish Socialist Party, statement of accounts for year ended 31st December 2012.
9. National Collective crowd-sourced £18,360 of funds and Radical Scotland crowd-sourced £2042 to finance leaflets for summer 2013.
10. Gordon Brown claimed this during the 2011 election campaign, saying, 'The SNP are utterly distracted by their obsession with independence' (Johnson, 2011)

http://www.telegraph.co.uk/news/uknews/scotland/scottish-politics/8489825/Scottish-Election-2011-Gordon-Brown-says-SNPs-obsession-with-independence-risks-recovery.html

11. BBC, 'Scottish election: Party leaders clash in BBC TV debate', 1 May 2011, http://www.bbc.co.uk/news/uk-scotland-scotland-politics-13255731
12. See for example Saltire magazine, Winter 2012, 'Edinburgh Agreement paves way for 2014 vote' and also Nicola Sturgeon, *Independence – a Renewed Partnership of the Isles*, Speech delivered at Edinburgh University, June 6 2013, http://www.scotland.gov.uk/News/Speeches/renewpartnership06052013
13. Alex Salmond, 'Voting Yes will create a new Scotland', *Saltire*, Winter 2012.
14. BBC, 2012, 'Scottish independence: One million Scots urged to sign 'yes' declaration', http://www.bbc.co.uk/news/uk-scotland-scotland-politics-18162832
15. Nicola Sturgeon, 'Bringing the powers home to build a better nation', speech delivered at Strathclyde University, 3 December 2012, http://www.scotland.gov.uk/News/Speeches/better-nation-031212
16. SNP, 2013, 'Moore comments branded more Project Fear nonsense', http://www.snp.org/media-centre/news/2013/jul/moore-comments-branded-more-project-fear-nonsense
17. SNP, 2013b, 'Scotland needs to make own choices', http://www.snp.org/media-centre/news/2013/aug/scotland-needs-make-own-choices

4

The Scottish Labour Party and the 2014 Independence Referendum

Eric Shaw

Introduction

This chapter offers an overview of the earlier phases of the Labour campaign, the so-called 'long campaign.' It is inevitably a partial account since the party anticipated that its campaign efforts would intensify in the Spring of 2014, with the all-important 'short campaign' only going into full swing in the summer. Like other parties Labour realised that it had to pace its activities, not only because of funding constraints but to avoid over-taxing the Scottish public's appetite for public debate. This chapter, after briefly discussing the context in which Labour formulated its thinking over the referendum, reviews its campaign strategy as it emerged in this early but formative stage. It then explores the crafting of its campaign message focusing on both the content and style of its campaigning effort. Finally it examines campaign techniques and decision-making before a brief conclusion.

The Evolution of Party Attitudes to the Autonomy Issue

Labour has been a long-standing, though not always consistent, advocate of devolution. The cause was first espoused by Keir Hardie in the 1880s. A generation later the 1918 party conference passed a resolution calling for devolution whilst in the following decade, Home Rule bills were introduced into the Commons by Labour MPs. But by the 1930s interest began to wane and the post-war Labour Government's creation of the welfare state solidified support behind the constitutional status quo. Interest in the issue revived in the 1970s, primarily as a result of the upsurge of support for the SNP which threatened Labour's Scottish bailiwick. In 1976 James Callaghan's government steered a devolution bill through the Commons only for it to be defeated at the 1979 referendum by the 40 per cent rule requirements

In truth, during this period, Labour was seriously divided over the issue. There were a number of outspoken advocates of devolution, notably John Mackintosh MP but it was stubbornly opposed, by constitutional conservatives on the right of the party and by many on the left who maintained that it was a distraction from efforts to foster the cause of socialism. However devolution began to regain momentum in the 1980s largely as resentment towards the social and economic changes imposed by the Thatcher Government spread. Opposition to Home Rule dwindled in Labour's ranks and under John Smith's leadership the party firmly pledged itself to legislating for devolution. This was enacted after Labour's 1997 election victory and confirmed by the referendum held later that year.

Under its first two parliaments (1999-2007) Scotland was ruled by a Labour-Liberal Democrat coalition under a succession of Labour First Ministers. However the Party's vote was on a downward slide and in 2007 it was ejected by the SNP which, winning a slightly larger proportion of the vote, was able to form a minority government. Four years later, after having been lulled by an unexpectedly solid performance at the 2010 Westminster election, Labour was crushed by the SNP which won an outright majority displacing its main rival from the position it had occupied for half-a-century as Scotland's premier party. The way was now clear for a referendum on independence.[1]

The referendum posed a series of problems and challenges for Labour. A brief comparison with the 1997 referendum will illustrate these. In 1997 the party had just received an overwhelming endorsement from the UK electorate whilst its mastery of the Scottish political scene was complete. It dominated Scotland's Westminster representation and was well entrenched in its local government bastions. In the intervening years much had changed. Whilst Labour's contingent in Westminster remained far more numerous than all other parties combined it had ceased to be Scotland's most popular party in Holyrood and the number of its councillors and of local authorities it controlled had steeply fallen, aided by changes to the electoral system for local government. Rightly or wrongly it was seen by many as a party in recession: the era of 'institutional Labour Scotland' was over (Hassan and Shaw, 2012).

A debate over independence raised other problems for Labour. It had been built upon the politics of class, community and trade unionism.

All of these had been progressively weakening for years and the ties that bound it to a large segment of the Scottish public began to unravel. Further, the party was operating within a milieu quite different from that of Westminster elections. Leaving aside the fact that a largely proportional electoral system ceased to flatter and inflate the party's strength, the central axis of party competition was between Labour and the SNP, with the latter able to appeal as effectively to the strong anti-Tory sentiment in Scotland as Labour. But the referendum was a vote that Labour could not afford to lose. The consequences of defeat were dire, far more so than for the Tories or Liberal Democrats. At risk for Scottish Labour MPs were their seats, their futures, their very careers. And at risk for the party was the prospect of winning what most anticipated would be a closely fought election in 2015.

Party Strategy for the Referendum

A useful way of outlining Labour's campaign strategy is by surveying the establishment, organisation and functions of three key institutions in the referendum debate, *Better Together, United with Labour* and the *Devolution Commission*. Better Together was the official umbrella organisation of the 'No' campaign, United with Labour was the party's own campaign vehicle whilst Labour's Devolution Commission was entrusted with formulating the party's 'constitutional offer'. We discuss each of the three bodies in turn.

Better Together was officially launched on June 2012 by Labour's former Chancellor of the Exchequer, the Edinburgh South MP Alastair Darling. A cross-party body, it encompassed all three of the pro-union parties (Labour, the Conservatives and the Liberal Democrats) as well as those affiliated to no party. Labour's leadership role, as by far the strongest party, was institutionally embedded. Darling, as chair of the five member Board of Directors was the chief spokesman and public face of the organisation. Of the four other members of the Board two were Labour representatives, Jackie Baillie MSP and Richard Baker MSP, with one each for the Conservatives and Liberal Democrats. In addition the influential Campaign Director of Better Together, Blair McDougall, had previously been a Labour political advisor (he also ran David Miliband's campaign for the Labour Party leadership).

It was a relatively well-funded and well-staffed body with a number of full time employees, including its Campaign Director, a Research and Engagement Officer and a National Campaign Organiser. These (and other) officials, working closely with the Board, were responsible for formulating campaign messages, and disseminating information, coordinating social media activities and arranging meetings. Considerable effort was given to briefing and training volunteers. For example in February 2014 a series of four worshops were organised across the country to provide training and advice on media management, doorstep canvassing, messaging and targeting voter pools (Better Together email 23 January 2014). Various sub-groups such as '[Armed] Forces Together' and 'Academics Together' were set up to mobilise support in what were seen to be influential sectors. Despite the potential for tension between bitterly divided parties Better Together operated in a consensual manner with few major disagreements. As one Labour insider commented 'We operate very closely together because we are all on the same side on this'.[2] Initially co-ordination between Better Together and the Labour Party was the responsibility of the Labour members of the Better Together Board and Anas Sarwar who headed up United with Labour. In July 2013, Drew Smith MSP was appointed by Johann Lamont as shadow minister for the newly-created Constitution portfolio charged with liaising with both Better Together and Anas Sarwar.

However the Better Together organisation, and the philosophy of cross-party collaboration it embodied, incurred criticism from within the Labour Party. The fact that Labour's Scottish Executive had not been consulted in advance about its creation hardly smoothed sensitivities.[3] A senior member, Jackson Cullinane (a Unite official and currently Party chair) objected that the party had been 'bounced' into the partnership and warned that contamination by the toxic Tory brand could come back 'to haunt Labour in electoral terms'. At a time when the Conservatives were imposing heavy public spending cuts many local activists, he warned, 'can't bring themselves' to work with the Tories (*Sunday Herald*, 17 November 2013). It was partly for this reason that Labour established a second body to campaign for a No vote, *United with Labour*.

Like Better Together, United with Labour was a leadership initiative though this time with the SEC's approval. It was launched in May 2013 by party leader Johann Lamont, deputy leader Anas Sarwar and Gordon Brown. Its primary functions were to operate as a vehicle for campaign activity by Labour activists, CLPs and trade unions reluctant to participate in the cross-party Better Together organisation and to formulate a distinctive Labour case. However it has not, as yet, acquired a substantial organizational presence with, at time of writing, little in the way of funds, resources and staff. Its major initiatives so far were confined to two major well-reported speeches by Gordon Brown, but little else. As a result United with Labour's impact was muted though this could change after the release of the Devolution Commission's report (see below) in early spring 2014. The relations between the two bodies avoided any significant friction with Anas Sarwar working closely with Better Together's two senior figures, Alistair Darling and Blair McDougall,[4] to co-ordinate their work. For example United with Labour concentrated its activities on grassroots activities in the west central belt, an area of traditional Labour strength where the party enjoyed more credibility than a cross-party group which included the Tories. Better Together, in turn, concentrated on reaching out to the voters via the media.

The third in the triad of bodies was Labour's Devolution Commission. Its origins lay in the deal reached following a Unite resolution at Scottish Labour's 2012 conference calling for a two-question referendum which would include a third option of enhanced devolution. The party leadership opposed the resolution and Unite agreed to side-line the resolution in return for the setting of a Commission which would investigate the devolution of fresh powers to Holyrood. Its mandate was to explore 'how can we meet the aspirations of the Scottish people for fuller devolution while maintaining the integrity of the UK which we know they value strongly?' (Devolution Commission, 2013: 7). The Commission's membership represented all the party's major stakeholders. It included two MSPs, Scottish Labour leader Johann Lamont and Duncan McNeil; three MPs, the Deputy Leader, Anas Sarwar, the Shadow Secretary of State for Scotland, Margaret Curran and the Shadow Minister for Work and Pensions, Gregg McClymont; Catherine Stihler MEP; Victoria Jamieson, Jackson Cullinane and Willie Young representing the CLPs, the unions and local government respectively. In July 2013 two more members were added, Drew Smith MSP (see above) and Sarah Boyack. So far, the Commission has not been troubled by sharp divisions of opinion though there have been significant strains between MPs and MSPs over the type, range and scope of the powers to be devolved.

The Commission's interim report, 'Powers for a purpose – strengthening devolution', was issued in April 2013 and it considered three major issues: the potential for fiscal autonomy, further policy devolution and for delegating power from Holyrood to local government. Its key proposal, on the fiscal front, was to consider the full devolution of income tax. This was chosen because it would raise a considerable amount of revenue, enable the Scottish Government to make the tax system more progressive, afford a wider range of fiscal choices and strengthen accountability. However it was a sensitive issue since MPs feared that it would further erode their role, standing and prestige. Another reservation, which featured in an early draft, was the danger of reviving the 'West Lothian question'. Transferring responsibility for income tax from Westminster to Holyrood would encourage the Tories to limit the right of Scottish MPs to participate in votes on the issues, hence further curtailing their powers (this was initially on page 48 of the draft report). This passage disappeared from the published draft. Furthermore the Commission was careful to state only that it was 'minded' to devolve the tax and to promise further consultation (Devolution Commission, 2013: 29). This by no means entirely dispelled opposition. A good number of MPs were unhappy and one frontbencher, Jim Murphy, complained to UK Labour leader Ed Miliband.

On welfare policy the report was generally unreceptive to proposals for further devolution. For example it insisted that pensions – a key reserved policy – should remain the responsibility of Westminster on the grounds that the Scottish people gained greater security by the pooling of resources and risks that membership of the UK entailed [a key argument for the Union made by Labour figures]. The Commission was more enthusiastic about devolving powers to local authorities and community organisations, an issue to which, despite its rather low salience in the public mind, considerable attention was granted. There were two main reasons for this. Firstly, it was Labour's response to pressure from councillors who resented what they saw as SNP-engineered centralisation of powers which had weakened local government. Secondly, it represented Labour's attempt to reframe debate from independence versus the Union to SNP centralisers versus Labour decentralizers.[5] Overall, the interim report contained few tangible policy recommendations but these, presumably, would come with the completion of the final report.

Scottish Labour's Campaign Message and Discourse at the Independence Referendum

Effective campaigning is all about crafting credible, plausible and appealing campaign messages. This is less (as used to be thought) about controlling the political agenda, more about a contest between rival political narratives (Stone, 1989). A political narrative is a representation of reality, a way of identifying and defining problems and of setting the lines of political division. The assumption underpinning this concept is that political realities are not given but constructed, and can be differentially activated. 'The social world' as Edelman put it, is 'a kaleidoscope of potential realities, any of which can be readily evoked by altering the ways in which observations are framed and categorized' (Edelman, 1993: 232).

The key mechanism is *framing*. 'To frame is to select some aspects of a perceived reality and make them more salient in a communicating text, in such a way as to promote a particular problem definition, causal interpretation, moral evaluation, and/or treatment recommendation for the item described' (Entman, 1993: 52). Frames help render issues, events or problems meaningful 'by simplifying and condensing aspects of the "world out there"' in ways that are 'intended to mobilize potential adherents and constituents, to garner bystander support, and to demobilize antagonists' (Snow and Benford, 1988: 198). From this perspective, the intrinsic qualities of issues or problems matter less than how they are construed. Framing, then, is about the competing efforts of rival parties to induce voters to accept their understanding of what is at stake, their representation of the issues and their definitions of the terms of debate. All parties to some degree engage in framing and narrative-formation but there are major variations in how sophisticated, complex and plausible they are. Equally, framing can be either 'negative' or 'positive' in style. It is to these issues that the next section turns.

The Negative Campaign

The 'No' campaign has frequently been assailed for its perceived negativity. One columnist condemned the Better Together campaign for its 'spiritual emptiness', its 'intellectual paucity' and 'its abject inability to produce anything that speaks of aspiration or hope or improvement if Scotland were to remain in the union' (Kevin McKenna, *Observer*, 1 December 2013). But the term 'negative campaigning' is very much a blanket one and needs to be disaggregated. Here we shall distinguish between three forms of negative campaigning, which will be called *critical, attack* and *anxiety-arousal*. Each has its distinct characteristics and purposes. Critical campaigning is about the critical scrutiny of an opponent's claims, policies and record. Attack campaigning seeks to tarnish the image, honesty, credibility and competence of senior figures in the opposing party. Anxiety-arousal is a form of campaigning which aims to deter people from voting by making them nervous, apprehensive and fearful about the consequences of the opponent's success.

To describe critical campaigning as 'negative' is to give a rather misleading impression of what it involved. Rather than assailing the opponent's case by denunciations or invective it involves subjecting it to critical analysis by reasoned argument, usually backed up by at least some evidence or factual material. It is negative insofar as it dwells upon the weaknesses and inconsistencies of the opposing party's case and the damaging effects of its policies if they were to be implemented

(Meyer, 1996: 441). It is an essential part of political debate. Given that Labour was seeking to mobilise support against a projected major political change it was inevitable that critical campaigning would form the core of Labour's argument. As transmitted mainly through Better Together this argument was framed in the following way. The intellectual case for an independent Scotland was poorly conceived, based on flimsy evidence and fundamentally unsound. Better Together formulated its case in terms of practicalities: the 'facts' – particularly the economic facts – and hard-headed calculation. The arguments presented by former Chancellor Alistair Darling – who had survived the financial crash with his reputation and credibility intact – were wide-ranging and often complex, but can be distilled into the following elements.

Firstly, the Scottish economy was inextricably intertwined with the UK economy and any 'separation' would be a wrenching and dislocating experience. Why 'turn our biggest market into our biggest competitor?' Scotland benefitted greatly from the union. For example, a mere 6 per cent of the products of its large insurance sector were sold in Scotland, compared to 94 per cent in the rest of the UK. Separation from the UK raised a real danger that major insurance companies would sooner or later relocate to where most of their business was conducted (Darling, November 2012).

Secondly, Labour and Better Together contended that independence would harm personal finances. For large numbers of undecided voters the referendum decision will not reflect perceptions of national identity, Better Together's communications officer, Ross MacRae, argued but rather 'a shrewd, practical decision – "what will this mean for me?" and most crucially "will I be better off"? Using (he claimed) IFS figures he warned that tax hikes alone would cost every basic rate taxpayer £1,000 per year on average[6] (*Progressonline*, 24 January 2014).

Thirdly, and more conceptually, Labour and Better Together questioned the reality of the SNP's quest for independence. The Nationalists now supported retention of the pound and a currency union with the rest of the UK, which meant that responsibility for monetary and exchange rate policy would be left in the hands of UK institutions. In what sense, then, could Scotland really be said to be sovereign? Not only would the Bank of England continue to set interest rates for Scotland, there would be no mechanism for the representation of Scottish interests. As the example of the Eurozone forcefully demonstrated a currency union, if it was to be sustainable, entailed sharp limits to economic sovereignty. Equally crucial, the Bank of England would continue to act as the lender of last resort – in effect, a foreign central bank would be performing this function essential for any nation-state. Furthermore, this raised the question of the whole point of independence. 'If', Darling contended, 'the purpose of independence is freedom for manoeuvre, to go your own way, why then hand back the levers of economic policy to your bigger next door neighbour which would by then be a foreign country'? (Darling, November 2012). In short, independence as envisaged by the SNP would be a self-defeating project for a currency union, which would lead 'inextricably towards political union, the very thing that Mr. Salmond wants to end in the UK' (Darling, *Financial Times*, 19 November, 2013).

The Attack Strategy

It has long been accepted in the literature on persuasive communication that in campaigns the issue of credibility is crucial. Research has consistently found that 'reactions to a communication are significantly affected by cues as to the communicators' intentions, expertness and trustworthiness', even where the message is the same (Hovland et al, 1953:35). As voter loyalties have become weaker and people more willing to switch parties, the issue of the credibility and competence of the key message givers – the party leaders – has swollen in importance. Scholars have distinguished between two elements of source credibility:

- Reliability: 'the extent to which a communicator is perceived to be a source of valid assertions'; and
- Trustworthiness: 'the degree of confidence in the communicator's intent to communicate the assertions he considers most valid' (Hovland et al, 1953:21).

For Scottish Labour, Alex Salmond was the Nationalist talisman, its most credible spokesman, the biggest asset in the campaign for independence. Strenuous efforts were made to discredit him. Attacks on Salmond's personality (his guile, duplicity and deceit) have been a part of the Labour-SNP battle for years, and were recently sharpened up. A recent focus of the referendum campaign was Salmond's relish for power, his vanity and conceit – with the suggestion that one of the reasons he supports independence is to satisfy his overweening ego. Examples given included most notably his widely-publicised unfurling of a Saltire at Andy Murray's Wimbledon victory. But the thrust of Labour's efforts here was to erode voter confidence in Salmond's probity and trustworthiness by highlighting his willingness, as a communicator, to play fast and loose with the facts. To take one example: the vexed question of an independent Scotland's membership of the EU. No one seriously doubted that the nation would eventually be accepted – the dispute was over the timing and ease of the process. Labour campaigners noted Salmond's assurances that Scotland would be automatically admitted into the EU, allegedly based on legal advice. But there was no such advice. To the contrary, European Commission President Jose Manuel Barroso, and other authoritative figures, made it clear that Scotland would have to take its place in the queue to negotiate entry (Alexander 2013). Equally, Ross MacRae, in a post entitled 'A question of trust' argued that the SNP had ought to suppress an internal paper revealing its plans – if and when Scotland became independent – to cut public sector job, old-age pension, freeze public spending and raise taxation (*Progressonline*, 17 October 2013). The message was simple: if Salmond and his colleagues misled the Scottish public on these issues how much credence could be given to his claims on others?

The Anxiety-arousal strategy

Critical campaigning interrogates the opponents' record and claims, attack campaigning seeks to impair or impugn their integrity. Anxiety-arousal campaigning, in contrast, operates on a more psychological, at times emotional level, seeking to influence the state of mind of the targeted audience. An anxiety-arousal strategy is a (diluted) version of a fear appeal, that is, 'a persuasive message that arouses fear by depicting a personally relevant and significant threat, followed by a description of feasible recommendations for deterring the threat' (Stiff, 1994: 120-1). This threat may or may not be genuine, accurately depicted or exaggerated. An effective anxiety-arousal appeal must also be a continuous process in that the receiver must be taught to respond to the anxiety-arousing and alleviating stimuli in a predictable and favourable manner (Hovland et al, 1953:62). Labour has used an anxiety-arousal strategy to foster a mood of disquiet, worry, even apprehension about the prospect of independence. Its campaign has revolved around the frequently-reiterated theme that independence constituted a perilous leap into the unknown; a gamble, a reckless step to take in an unpredictable and threatening world. The Union, Darling recalled, had afforded Scotland 'security against risks': when its two leading banks collapsed it was able to call upon the resources of the whole of the UK. Left alone and isolated, Scotland would have been much more vulnerable with potentially debilitating consequences (Darling, 2013:17). Labour did not deny Scotland's ability to survive as an independent nation. The point was that it would become less secure, less shielded if separated from the UK. For example, No campaigners seized upon a report by the highly-respected Institute for Fiscal Studies stating that large tax rises or spending cuts would be unavoidable to defray the pension costs of a population aging more rapidly than that of the UK as a whole (Martin Wolf, *Financial Times*, 21 November, 2013).

The SNP has consistently sought to alleviate fears about the economic consequences of independence from the UK by pointing to the availability of ample oil revenues – a central plank in the case for independence. Labour's strategy here was predicated on emphasising the degree to which, far from being a fail-safe and reliable asset, North Sea oil was a volatile commodity. This narrative stressed the unpredictability of oil revenue because of sharp fluctuations in oil prices and the likelihood of steadily falling oil production. Was it not hasty and ill-advised to rely so heavily on so fickle a stream of income? This would compound the problems of a larger budget deficit, loss of investor confidence, tax rises and spending cuts a newly independent Scotland would inevitably face (Darling, *Huffington Post*, 3 October 2013).

Not only would quitting the Union increase Scotland's exposure to capricious international forces, a decision to vote 'yes' was irrevocable, 'a one way ticket to a deeply uncertain destination' (Darling, 10 November 2012). At this time of straitened economic circumstances, and widespread anxieties about jobs and living standards membership of the UK brought 'certainty at a time of insecurity' (Darling, July 2013:6). Why jeopardise this? 'With so much uncertainty and unanswered questions about the cost of independence' would not leaving the UK, Darling asked, 'be a huge leap in the dark'? (Darling, 26 November 2013).

Scotland, the Union and Social Democracy

A positive campaign is one that appeals to the voters on the basis of what a party stands for, its policies, ideals and aspirations. The referendum was not a normal campaign in that the issue was a simple constitutional proposition. But both sides feared that a campaign that dwelt mainly on constitutional intricacies – simply the pros and cons of independence – would rapidly tire most voters. In the Labour dictum 'powers had to be for a purpose', that is, for the realization of some larger social vision. The crucial dividing line between Labour and the Conservatives (the economy aside) has normally been the size, shape and governance of the welfare state. In Scotland, in contrast, there is a broad measure of agreement between Labour and the SNP on such matters. Since each claim was animated by similar ideals – social justice, equity and social solidarity – the debate was less over the desirability of these aspirations than whether they can best be advanced by independence or the union. James Mitchell has argued that 'The traditional appeal of the Union for many Scots lay in the social welfare afforded by successive UK governments. (....). If Scots believe the welfare state is being dismantled, then one of the most important pillars of the union will be removed' (Mitchell, 2013). The SNP's case was that it was being dismantled by the Tories and their governmental allies, and that the most effective way to safeguard it was through independence.

Labour responded to the SNP's bid to occupy its traditional ideological territory by questioning the genuineness of its allegiance to social democratic values. The SNP government may have, (as one MSP put it) 'a wonderful policy framework', but it has not furnished the funds to put it into effect. Its rhetoric was not matched by its deeds.[7] Further, it was riddled with contradictions. On the one hand, it has pledged to preserve high-quality public services whilst, on the other, it has (to attract corporate support) promised reductions in taxation. Salmond's pledge to cut Corporation Tax became emblematic of this. This would set in motion, Labour argued, a 'race to the bottom', causing a loss of tax revenues and thereby squeezing the finances needed to fund public services (Brown, 2 September 2013; Devolution Commission, 2013:25, 9). Labour repeatedly quoted Nobel prize-winner (and member of The SNP's Fiscal Commission Working Group) Joe Stiglitz's observation that: 'Some of you have been told that lowering tax rates on corporations will lead to more investment. The fact is that's not true. It is just a gift to corporations increasing inequality in our society' (*Scotland on Sunday*, 29 January 2014). As Anas Sarwar put it, the SNP promises 'Scandinavian public services, but the tax system of Monaco. That's not honest and not credible' (Sarwar, 26 November 2013).

Persuasive efforts are likely to be more effective if rather than seeking to alter attitudes they focus on changing perceptions of the situation to which people are responding (McGuire, 1989:56). This is where framing strategies play a key role. Labour reframed the constitutional issue in terms of sustaining the 'social union' [though so did the SNP]. The UK-wide welfare state allowed the pooling of resources and risks 'across a larger and more resilient political and economic community' than that would be available to Scotland alone (Scottish Labour Devolution Commission, 2013:38). Thus resources have been redistributed from the areas of greatest wealth (such as the South East) to the areas of greatest need (such as parts of Scotland and the North East of England) (Darling, 2013:24, 26; Brown, 2 September 2013).

These were the bare outlines of Labour's positive campaign but many of the details were yet to be filled in at the time of writing. The purpose of the Devolution Commission's report, due to be published in March 2014, was to provide a fuller view of Labour's proposed new constitutional settlement and a clearer indication of how the party's broader social goals (yet to be fully specified) will be facilitated by a further instalment of devolution.

Who do you think you are? Questions of Identity

Social identity – defined by class, religion, ethnicity or some other characteristic – has long been acknowledged as a key factor in shaping political behaviour. Social identity can here be defined as an individual's 'knowledge that he belongs to a certain social group together with some emotional and value significance of his membership' (Tajfel and Forgas, 1981:124). Whilst the impact of class identity has tended to wane, that of identities rooted in region, ethnicity and nationhood have generally flourished. People, of course, have multiple identities: the key question is their relative salience and the effect this has on how they see themselves, on their image of the social order and of the constellation of interests of which it is composed. National identity has long been seen as a politically significant issue in Scotland. Scots are regularly polled about the degree to which they identify themselves as British and Scottish or some amalgam of the two. The issue of identity has become a salient one in the referendum campaign because it is commonly assumed (not least by Labour campaigners) that the more voters see themselves as exclusively Scottish and frame the referendum issue in terms of competing Scottish/English interests and identities then the more likely they will vote for independence.

The nature of the relationship between social identify and political preferences is a complex issue. At one time that relationship was defined in a clear-cut way, e.g. people who defined themselves as working class would more or less automatically vote Labour. Now the relationship is understood in more complex ways. Firstly there is a general recognition that people have several identities: what matters, in terms of electoral behaviour, is which is more forcefully evoked. For Labour, the danger in the referendum debate was that where intense Scottish identities were stimulated 'heart' would prevail over 'head'; that is to say that the sense of pride in being Scottish – pride in Scottish history, traditions values and customs – would spill over into enthusiasm for the cause of independence. Labour's response was to refute the notion that Scottish patriotism could only be expressed by backing independence. Identities were multiple and inclusive: 'as Scots', Better Together proclaimed, 'we all feel proudly Scottish but most of us also feel at least a bit British. We don't have to choose between the two... None of us feel any less Scottish just because we are part of a bigger United Kingdom' (http://bettertogether.net/pages/about). In Darling's words, it is 'entirely possible to be a patriotic Scot and be wholly at ease with being British' (Darling, 2013:22).

More generally the way in which identity effects electoral choice is mediated by its impact on how people see themselves, define their interests, perceive which groups are at odds over a particular issue and in general orient themselves to the political world. An activated social identity, in short, not only invokes a sense of who you are but also operates as an interpretive framework influencing how one defines and apprehends political issues. 'Depending upon the particular group identity one assumes in reacting to an issue, ideas and feelings about it may be produced and organized in different ways' (Price, 1989: 202). The frame deployed by the SNP, Labour contended, construed political relations between Scotland and the rest of the UK in terms of competing national interests, identities and aspirations. This – the argument ran – engendered a distorted understanding of the challenges and problems confronting Scotland. These were no different from those faced by the rest of the UK: unemployment, poverty, stagnating living standards, struggling public services and rampant inequality. The common interest in overcoming injustice and inequality transcended national identity. Ordinary Scots had far more in common with ordinary people in Manchester or Sunderland than they do with the well-heeled Edinburgh banker. 'We don't fight England', Labour's Scottish leader declared, 'We fight social injustice. And that crosses borders... We believe in solidarity. We stand with our neighbours. Not just out of sentiment but because it makes sense for us all' (Lamont, May 2013). As one senior Labour figure insisted 'the politics of separation is not the way to create political change.' Indeed the politics of nationalism was having a reactionary effect because it sowed divisions between Scottish and English workers who shared common interests and values.[8]

There were those within the party, on the left and within the unions organised loosely in the Red Paper Collective who urged that Labour should formulate an explicitly class-based analysis of the problem facing Scotland (Bryan and Kane, 2013). Class analysis and a grasp of the dynamics of capitalism should operate as the prism through which to view Scotland's problems and opportunities. The argument here, in its essentials, was that 'political mobilisation has to be conceived and constructed at a British level'. The ownership of productive resources, the conduits for the extraction of wealth from labour, the key linkages between big business and political power all operated at a British level and none would be altered by independence (Watson, 2013:10-11),

Politics was about class, not nationality. 'Posing nation against class' Unison official Dave Watson and a Red Paper author declared, 'is a blind alley which will only reinforce the country's exposure to the power of multinational capitalism' (Watson, 2013:13). The Labour leadership stopped short of framing the issues in this way, partly because they were few in the uppermost reaches of the party who accepted this model of politics and partly because it would be unacceptable to the party's partners in Better Together. Hence the terms 'class' and 'socialism' rarely figured in Labour's official rhetoric – least of all any notion of class struggle – and to the extent that references were made to shared class interests across the borders it was in a rather restrained and tepid fashion. Instead it utilized a more muted and vague appeal to trans-territorial interests and alignments which appealed to the cause of social justice, solidarity and greater equality and for which modifying constitutional arrangements was an irrelevant distraction.[9]

Labour's Campaign: Techniques and Decisionmaking

What campaign techniques has Labour used? Much has been made of the advanced techniques now routinely deployed by political parties. Instead of the old-style doorstep campaigning (canvassing, leafleting, meetings, etc.) parties now employ more capital-intensive methods which call upon the (normally paid) skills of polling experts, image consultants, marketing and advertising executives. The major forum for electioneering is no longer the constituency but the national news media, now supplemented with increasing utilization of the internet and the new social media. Methodical and extensive use is made of public opinion research to monitor shifts in public attitudes, test slogans and soundbites and in formulating campaign messages (Farrell and Webb, 2002). Surprisingly, Labour's campaign appeared to buck these trends. Evidence culled at time of writing (January 2014) suggested that it had relied primarily on grass-roots, community-based activities staffed largely by local activists. Penetration of the local milieu, rather than media-focused efforts to reach the electorate as a whole, was seen as crucial to both identifying potential sympathisers and getting the message across. 'Grassroots campaigning' one senior MSP explained, 'had to be a priority. We need to know where the vote is to turn it out. We need to know where the undecided are to target them'.[10] Trusted local opinion-formers, people well-known and highly-regarded within their communities played a key role. Voters were more likely to be attentive to those with whom they could relate. Far from being superceded, as one leading figure put it, Labour campaigners were for the most part convinced that 'street campaigning does work'.[11]

Television and the press seemed (so far) to have played a somewhat smaller role than one might have anticipated. In part this may be because Scottish Labour inhabits a more benign media environment than its British counterpart. It does not confront, as its UK-wide counterpart does, relentless assaults from a pugnaciously hostile press. On the specific issue of independence it could rely on broad sympathy from the bulk of the press and assiduous efforts to influence its coverage were not seen as a priority. It is difficult to establish the precise use made of outside professionals such as opinion pollsters, marketing advisors and public relations consultants. However it is unlikely to have been extensive largely because of resource constraints – though this may to some degree change during the 'short' campaign. Only a modest degree of opinion research, it seems, was commissioned, mostly by Better Together, but it is unclear how data culled from such research was fed into the campaign. Finally, and as far as one can judge, Labour was not using the new social media to any great extent beyond communicating with its supporters and organising its activities.

Who was responsible for designing and implementing campaign strategy? In theory the Scottish Executive is entrusted with the administration and overall direction of the party, the Scottish Policy Forum for policy formation over devolved issues and the Scottish Conference for final decision-making. In reality matters are less clear-cut. For example the SEC was not consulted over the setting up of Better Together and was only tangentially involved in strategic decision-making. Similarly, United with Labour fits uneasily into party structures with rather vague lines of accountability. As one party official noted 'my impression is that it is a free-standing campaign run by Anas [Sarwar]'.[12] Again, though in theory it has the task of developing Labour policy, the Scottish Policy Forum did not have any institutionalised input into the work of the Devolution Commission.[13] Equally the relationship and lines of responsibility between Labour's Scottish Executive and the Devolution Commission seem not to have been thought through.[14]

With whom, then, does real power lie? Inevitably, a key role is played by the party leader, Johann Lamont, and her closest advisors and frontbench colleagues. This reflected the process evident in most parties by which power has been transferred from the party organisation and the 'party on the ground' to the parliamentary leadership (Katz and Mair, 2002:128-9). However it would be wrong to conclude that control over decision-making is confined to a narrow and cohesive elite.

In fact, it remains diffused: the assent or at least acquiescence of key stakeholders, including senior MSPs, MPs, frontbenchers, affiliated trade is generally required before major initiatives are launched. There are, in the words of one Holyrood frontbencher 'very many complex relationships which are all forums for ironing disagreements'.[15] Perhaps the most important institution was the recently-established Management Board bringing together the leader of the Scottish party, the deputy leader and the Shadow Secretary of State for Scotland. One frontbencher commented 'If I was pushed to say which is key decision-making body, it is this'.[16] Lamont's personal advisers, notably her senior spin doctor, Paul Sinclair, also exerted considerable influence behind the scenes.

What of the rank and file? The Scottish Policy Forum was dormant during this period and was effectively side-lined. However some attempts were made to draw members into the work of the Devolution Commission. An open consultation was held on the interim report with facilities for members to respond online via the website, by e-mail or by post. The Commission also sought to elicit comments from trade unions and local Councils. At time of writing (January 2014) the response rate was relatively low but this may have changed in time How comments and responses from party bodies will be processed and how much impact they will have on the Commission's final report was yet to be seen. What, then, of the role of the UK party? Despite the fact that for Scottish Labour MPs the stakes were high – 41 will have their political life cut brutally short if 'Yes' triumphed – the British leadership agreed that the campaign was primarily the responsibility of the Scottish leadership and adopted a low profile.[17] Institutional differences (especially over the scale and desirability of further devolution) might divide MPs and MSPs but strenuous efforts were made to manage these differences, or at least to keep them out of the public eye, through continual dialogue. Both sets of political actors had too much to lose.

The Unions and the Campaign

One overlooked aspect of the campaign was the role of the trade unions. Ever since the party's formation the unions have played a major role in Labour campaigning, supplying funds, personnel, office-space and telephone facilities. Despite its critical importance for the party the campaign for the 'No' vote received considerably less support than might have been expected. The three largest unions in Scotland (as in the UK) are Unite, Unison and GMB – unions which North of the border tend to work closely together. Only the GMB, the smallest of the three, pledged to campaign alongside Labour for a No vote. This lack of support from what are the party's two largest affiliates for a major election is almost unprecedented. All three unions are represented on the SEC and one official (Jackson Cullinane of Unite) joined the Devolution Commission. However, only the GMB has agreed to commit resources to United with Labour. In a press release in November 2013 the union's political officer, Richard Leonard, stated that the union membership had been consulted and strongly favoured rejecting independence.[18] He concluded that 'We couldn't in all conscience sit on the fence for the next ten and a half months' (Leonard, 2013) – but this is precisely what Unite and Unison (so far) opted to do. At time of writing, Unite was conducting a wide-ranging consultation of members whose views will be fed into the Regional Committee charged with taking a final decision. Anticipating there will be no clear view either way, the Regional Committee refused to commit to either side, for two major reasons. Firstly, neither side had given sufficiently convincing answers to major questions on a range of issues, such as employment law and pensions. Secondly, and more importantly, the union was unwilling to run the risk of divisions – which might persist long after the referendum – over a constitutional question which did not impinge on its prime purposes.[19] Unison took a broadly similar view, declaring that it was not its role 'to promote or condemn the politics of national identity, Scottish or British. We should not accept at face value any of the claims from any side of the constitutional debate' (Unison, 2012).

It is difficult to determine precisely why the three unions have reached sharply differing conclusions. One possibility is differences in sectoral interests. But these affect all unions and it may be there are internal political factors at work. Whatever the truth of the matter, there has been no interference by the UK leaderships of the two unions, both of which had pledged to abide by the decisions of their Scottish wing.[20] Of more bearing to the campaign are the consequences. Although United with Labour was set up in part at the instigation of the unions, neither of the largest, Unite or Unison, will participate in its work. In effect these two unions, which have contributed so much to Labour campaigns over the years, will be on the side-lines: there will be no donations nor any other resources for the 'No' campaign.[21]

Conclusion

At this point in time it is difficult to make any definite statement about Labour's campaign overall: its quality, coherence and effectiveness. However, its main characteristics are clear enough. It is double-pronged, with Labour campaigning both in a cross-party alliance (Better Together) and independently (United with Labour). There has been some criticism about the negativity of its campaign, especially that conducted by Better Together, but we have suggested that this is simplistic and to a degree misleading. Given that Labour inevitably has to subject to critical analysis the claim that independence will benefit Scotland it is bound, to some degree, to be seen to be 'negative'. On the other hand there are elements in Labour's campaign which do correspond to the more conventional meaning of 'negative': its efforts to demolish the credibility of the 'Yes' campaign and its use of anxiety-arousal techniques. Campaigning is about the contest between rival narratives; about shaping how voters define events and conditions by assigning meanings to them, and then using frames to transmit those meanings to voters. In the case of the Scottish referendum this has included the debate over the content and implications of contested political concepts such as identity, independence and democracy. Narratives also have normative aspects. Thus the GMB union called for 'a credible, compelling and distinctive Scottish Labour vision for an equal and democratic country' (Leonard, 2013). So far Labour had spoken in rather vague language about a future Scotland defined by fairness and social justice but these values lacked definition and detail and it was not always clear how they would be translated into action. This, however, could change (as noted) with the unveiling of its Devolution Commission report and with the launch of the decisive 'short campaign' in the summer of 2014. Only with the final vote will we know which of the rival narratives have resonated more with the popular mind.

Note

This chapter has relied heavily on interviews conducted with seven senior figures from the Scottish Labour party and trade unions, mostly on an off-the-record basis and I would like to thank them for their help and generosity with their time. I would also like to thank the two Labour party officials who read the whole of an earlier draft of this chapter and made some very valuable suggestions.

References

Alexander, Douglas (2013), 'Walking Away From Others Has Never Been the Scottish Way', *Huffington Post*, 17 October 2013.

Benford, R. and Snow, D. (2000), ' Framing Processes and Social Movements: An Overview and Assessment', *Annual Review of Sociology*, Vol. 26, pp. 611–639.

Bennett, W. and Edelman, M. (1985), 'Homo Narrans: Toward a New Political Narrative', *Journal of Communication*, Vol. 35, No. 4.

Brown, Gordon (2013) *A positive, principled and forward-looking case for the union*, athttp://www.scottishlabour.org.uk/blog/entry/a-positive-principled-and-forward-looking-case-for-the-union, 2 September 2013.

Bryan, P. and Kane, T. (2013), *Class, Nation and Socialism: The Red Paper on Scotland*, Glasgow, Glasgow Caledonian Archives.

Darling, Alistair [2012], '*Better Together*', John P Mackintosh lecture, 10 November 2012.

Darling, Alistair (2013), *We Belong Together: The case for a United Kingdom*, University of Glasgow, July 2013, http://b.3cdn.net/better/8e048b7c5f09e96602_jem6bc28d.pdf

Darling, Alistair (2013), *Oil Volatility Means Cuts or Tax Rises for Scotland*, Huffington Post, 3 October 2013, at http://www.huffingtonpost.co.uk/alistair-darling/scottish-independence-oil-revenue_b_4031754.html

Darling, Alistair (2013), 'What does independence even mean for Scotland?', *Financial Times*, 19 November 2013.

Darling, Alistair [2013], 'Nothing has changed" – Darling responds to SNP White Paper on Independence', *Labour List*, 26 November 2013.

Edelman, Murray (1993), 'Contestable categories and public opinion', *Political Communication*, Vol. 10 No. 3, pp. 231–242.

Entman, R M (1993), 'Framing: Towards Clarification of a Fractured Paradigm' *Journal of Communication*, Vol. 43 No.4.

Farrell, D. and Webb, P. (2002), 'Political Parties as Campaign Organizations', in Dalton, R and Wattenberg [Eds], *Parties Without Partisans: Political Change in Advanced Industrial Democracies*, Oxford, Oxford University Press.

Hassan, G and Shaw, E (2012), The *Strange Death of Labour Scotland*, Edinburgh, Edinburgh University Press.

Hovland, C., Janis, I. and Kelley, H. (1953), *Communication and Persuasion*, New Haven, Yale University Press.

Katz, R. and Mair, P. (2002), 'The Ascendancy of the Party in Public Office' in Gunther, R., Montero J. and Linz J. [Eds], *Political Parties: Old concepts and New Challenges*, Oxford, Oxford University Press.

Lamont , Johann (May, 2013), Speech at United with Labour launch, 13 May 2013, at http://www.scottishlabour.org.uk/blog/entry/united-with-labour-launch-speech-by-johann-lamont-msp-leader-of-the-scottis

Leonard, Richard (2013), 'GMB Scotland to campaign for a "No" vote in independence referendum', November 2013, at http://www.scottishlabour.org.uk/blog/entry/gmb-scotland-campaigning-for-a-no-vote

McGuire, W. [1989], 'Theoretical foundations of campaigns', in Rice R. and Paisley W. (Eds.), *Public Communication Campaigns*, Beverly Hills, California, Sage.

McDougall, Blair [2013], 'Bloodless revolution', posted on *Progressonline*, 30 September 2013.

Meyer, W. (1996), 'In Defense of Negative Campaigning', *Political Science Quarterly*, Vol. 111, No. 3, pp. 437-455.

Mitchell, James [2013], 'How the SNP can still win the vote for an independent Scotland' *Guardian*, 16 October, 2013.

Price, V. (1989), 'Social Identification and Public Opinion: Effects of Communicating Group Conflict', *Public Opinion Quarterly*, Vol. 53, No. 2, pp. 197–224.

Sarwar, Anas [2013], speech at United with Labour launch, 13 May 2013.

Sarwar, Anas 2013], 'Is that it?: The SNP White paper on Independence', *Labour List*, 26 November 2013.

Scottish Labour Devolution Commission (2013), *Powers for a purpose – strengthening devolution, Interim Report*, Glasgow, Scottish Labour Party, April 2013.

Snow, D. and Benford, R. [1988], 'Ideology, Frame Resonance, and Participant Mobilization', *International Social Movement Research*, Vol. 1, pp. 197–217.

Stiff, J. [2002], *Persuasive Communication*, New York, Guilford Press.

Stone, D. (1989), 'Causal Stories and the Formation of Policy Agendas', *Political Science Quarterly*, Vol. 104, No. 2, pp. 281-300.

Tajfel, S. and Forgas, J. (1982), 'Social categorisation: cognitions, values and groups', in Forgas, J. (Ed.), *Social Cognition*, New York, Academic Press.

Unison (2012), *A Fairer Scotland*, Unison Scotland, at http://www.unison-scotland.org.uk/scotlandsfuture/FairerScotlandNov2012.pdf

Watson, D (2013), 'Class not Nation', *Scottish Left Review* 78, Sept./Oct 2013.

Notes

1. It is worth noting the approval by the Scottish Parliament of the Labour-instigated Commission on Scottish Devolution, chaired by Sir Kenneth Calman which reported in 2009. This recommended vesting Holyrood with a range of new powers, most importantly over income tax. This was approved by both parliaments through the Scotland Act which came into force in 2012.
2. Interview with author.

3. Interview with author.
4. If there was, one Labour insider commented 'I would love to know' (interview)
5. Interview with author.
6. Interestingly this figure – £1000 – was the same as that rolled out by the Tories as the cost per taxpayer of Labour's plans at the 1987 and 1992 elections.
7. Interview with author.
8. Interview with author.
9. Interview with author.
10. Interview with author.
11. Interview with author.
12. Interview with author.
13. Interview with author.
14. Interview with author.
15. Interview with author.
16. Interview with author.
17. Interview with author.
18. He explained: 'The current balance of economic forces we face dictates that we should not breakaway and withdraw but actively engage at the level where power, especially economic power, lies' (Leonard, 2013).
19. Interview with author.
20. Interviews with author.
21. Interview with author.

5

The Scottish Conservatives and the 2014 Independence Referendum

David Torrance

Introduction

As the party that took longest to adjust to the realities of a devolved Scotland, the Scottish Conservative *and Unionist* Party (to give it its full title) entered the independence referendum campaign in a frame of mind at once clear and resolute, but also in a state of flux. The former because it was unequivocal in its support for 'the Union', but more open minded in terms of what came next. This parallel approach had largely been shaped by the party's recent – and generally poor – electoral performance. Particularly weak results in the 2010 and 2011 elections had finally nudged the Scottish Tory leadership into living a little more dangerously on the constitutional front.

Even beyond the Scottish Parliament, its political position was weak. Although the largest part of the UK Coalition government it had just one MP north of the border, the Scotland Office minister David Mundell, and thus its place in the cross-party 'Better Together' campaign was a junior one. Acutely aware of voter perceptions (generally hostile) Scottish Conservatives were content to play second fiddle to the Scottish Labour Party in the 28 month-long referendum campaign, but at the same time the party's leadership viewed September 2014 as an opportunity to rebuild support and boost the profile of its new leader, Ruth Davidson. Indeed, the referendum acted as a focal point for several party strategies: organisational, leadership and constitutional. The prospect of a vote on independence concentrated minds throughout Scotland's political class, not least its oldest 'Unionist' party.

But while Labour and the Liberal Democrats could draw upon long devolutionary backstories (the former had created the Scottish Parliament in 1999; the latter were, broadly speaking, federalist), the last time Conservatives in Scotland had done any serious thinking about the constitution had been in the late 1960s and 1970s. This chapter charts the evolution of Conservative Party attitudes towards the Union over the past century, assesses its approach to the independence referendum, analyses the language used by the party – in both Edinburgh and London – to communicate its constitutional objectives, looks at the influence of multi-level politics on its performance and, finally, asks if a decisive 'no' vote in September 2014 might offer the party scope to reverse its historic decline.

The evolution of Scottish Conservative attitudes towards autonomy

Conservative Party attitudes towards constitutional change have been little charted and much caricatured. From 1885, when Lord Salisbury (in concert with his Liberal opponents) sanctioned the creation of a 'Scottish Office', until 1968 when Edward Heath committed his party to establishing a 'Scottish Assembly', it emphasised *administrative* rather than *legislative* devolution, a good example of what Graeme Morton called 'Unionist Nationalism' [Morton, 1999]. Until 1922 this occurred within the context of a strongly stated opposition to Irish independence, but after the formation of the Irish Free State the party's 'Unionism' was increasingly assumed to refer to the 1707 Anglo-Scottish Union rather than that of 1800/1801. Therefore, Heath's 'Declaration of Perth' was significant, for the Conservatives became the first mainstream UK political party to back devolution, and while this is generally depicted as out of character, Margaret Arnott and Catriona M. M. Macdonald viewed it as 'less of an aberration' and more of a 'missed opportunity to take a long-held commitment to administrative devolution all the way to a legislative end' [Arnott and Macdonald, 2012:45].

Indeed, Heath's pledge suffered death by a thousand cuts, mainly a consequence of his later government's inaction and his successor's downright hostility. Margaret Thatcher's priority was to prevent a split, her Scottish party being divided between those who supported devolution (some styled themselves the 'Thistle Group' in the late 1960s) and those who viewed it as a slippery slope towards dissolution of the Union. And although many Tories were involved in the formal 'no' campaigns during the 1979 referendum on a Scottish Assembly, Mrs

Thatcher's position remained supportive of devolution (in principle), just not the model proposed by James Callaghan's government; the 1979 Conservative Party manifesto committing the party to 'discussions about the future government of Scotland' with the SNP, Labour and Liberals [Conservative Party, 1979].

But having won the 1979 general election, Thatcher took that and the inconclusive result of the referendum as proof the Scottish Question had been satisfactorily answered. By the time of Tony Blair's 1997 landslide election victory, Conservative views of devolution had become if anything more hostile and inflexible. In the second devolution referendum that followed, the party's 'Think Twice' 'no' campaign, poorly funded and hastily assembled, did not stand a chance against the cross-party 'Scotland Forward' coalition of Labour, the SNP and Liberal Democrats. The public mood favoured change and the Scottish Conservative Party simply succeeded in consolidating perceptions of itself as 'anti-Scottish'.

Even once the Scottish Parliament was established in 1999, eighteen newly-elected Conservative MSPs often appeared grudging participants in the new political order. David McLetchie (1952-2013), the MSP group's first leader, concentrated on the party's core vote, although that often involved criticising the new institution, particularly the controversy surrounding its new home at Holyrood. Senior party figures urged him to consider a bold commitment to fiscal autonomy, but fearful of splitting the party McLetchie resisted [Torrance, 2012]. Annabel Goldie, who became leader in 2005, pursued the same strategy of 'safety first' in terms of the constitution, although senior figures – most notably Murdo Fraser and Brian Monteith – periodically floated the idea of fiscal autonomy, and even federalism.

Following the election of a minority SNP Scottish Government in May 2007 Scottish Conservative strategy shifted in two important respects. First of all the party attempted to 'detoxify' by co-operating with the SNP in the Scottish Parliament, supporting its budgets in return for policy concessions, while also co-operating with the other Unionist parties – Labour and the Liberal Democrats – in formulating a scheme for greater devolution via the cross-party Calman Commission. Although both caused internal tensions and unhappiness among the party grassroots, the leadership calculated that it would demonstrate the party's 'relevance' in terms of domestic policy and in the context of the constitutional debate, which enjoyed renewed vigour given the SNP's commitment to holding a referendum on independence.

To this, however, the Conservatives remained opposed, and attempts by the Scottish Government to introduce the relevant legislation did not progress given the clear determination of all three Unionist parties to block it. Occasional Tory voices did advocate calling the SNP's bluff by actually supporting a referendum, for example the former Conservative MSPs Phil Gallie and David Davidson, and Lord Forsyth, the last Conservative Secretary of State for Scotland. 'We should get on with it and put it to the people,' he told a Sunday newspaper. 'If people want to get out of the United Kingdom so be it. Otherwise let's get on with dealing with the enormous problems' [Allardyce, 2009].

Although this was not a mainstream view, the election of David Cameron as UK Conservative Party leader in 2005 had also changed the party's approach to the constitutional question. Relatively free of his predecessors' baggage, he supported the Calman process as Leader of the Opposition and, on becoming Prime Minister in May 2010, consented to it taking legislative form via the Scotland Bill. Cameron also pushed what his sole MP David Mundell called the 'respect agenda', making a point of visiting Alex Salmond in Edinburgh within a week of forming his Coalition Government. All of this represented a significant break with the approach of previous Conservative governments, but public opinion remained hostile; opponents, meanwhile, cast the Coalition in predictable terms, particularly as it started to cut public spending.

Although the party's attitude towards devolution was not part of its remit, the Sanderson Commission on the future of the Scottish Conservative and Unionist Party – appointed following a disappointing election result in May 2010 – said it could not 'ignore the quantity of submissions on whether or not Scotland should have greater fiscal accountability', recommending it be 'discussed fully between both the Scottish Conservatives and the UK party, as well as forming the basis of a fully informed debate within the party membership'. But the main point of the review was to assess what it frankly called the party's 'moribund' local associations and 'weak' leadership structures.

The key recommendation, therefore, was the election of a 'distinctly Scottish leader' who could command the whole Scottish party rather than just its MSP group. More widely, the review admitted that Scots remained unclear as to 'what the Scottish Conservatives stand for', except that it was still considered to be 'anti-Scottish' [Sanderson, 2010]. These themes dominated discussion of the party's tactics – and indeed prospects – in the run up to the 2011 Holyrood elections, in which the party registered its worst ever result, 13.9 and 12.4 per cent of the constituency and list votes respectively, enough to elect just 15 MSPs, five fewer than anticipated following positive boundary changes. Within weeks of the result Annabel Goldie had announced her resignation as Scottish Tory leader.

Party strategy for the referendum

Thus, in the aftermath of May 2011, the Scottish Conservative Party's search for a new leader inevitably dovetailed with its strategy for handling a referendum on independence that, with the election of a majority SNP government, now appeared inevitable. The party's previous attempt to emphasise an enhanced devolution settlement via the Calman Commission and Scotland Bill had clearly been overtaken by events. Blocking a Referendum Bill in the Scottish Parliament was no longer an option.

Initially, however, the party lacked clear direction at any level. As the Conservative-led Coalition considered how to respond to the SNP's victory, the party in Scotland got down to electing a successor to Annabel Goldie, a process that prompted a thorough discussion (public and private) of the challenges it faced at a number of levels. Murdo Fraser, previously a hard-line Unionist, had – at the party's 2011 spring conference – begun to repudiate his and others' previous warnings about the likely effect of devolution, making the point that the 'slippery slope' argument had been wrong in 1997-99 and was therefore wrong again in the context of a debate about endowing Holyrood with greater powers. There was a memorable showdown between Fraser and his former mentor Lord Forsyth on this issue at the 2011 Scottish Conservative Party conference.

Launching his leadership bid several months later, Fraser built on this by arguing that the Scottish Conservatives had to 'see the referendum on independence not as a threat, but as an opportunity'. He continued:

> We are united and unwavering in our determination to preserve the United Kingdom. But the way we choose to campaign to save the United Kingdom will say much about us. Just as our opposition to devolution throughout the 1980s and 1990s defined us then. So, our approach to Scotland's constitutional future in the 2010s will define us now. Our early opposition to the Scottish Parliament has led to us being portrayed as anti-Scottish. And, whether we like it or not, that is still the perception of much of the Scottish electorate. To counter it, we need both an admission and a reality-check. Painful as it may be for us to admit, our analysis of the impact of devolution was overstated. The idea that devolution is inevitably a slippery slope to separation. And that any power devolved is a step closer to independence. Such a message was too simplistic.

A 'New Unionism', he suggested, would 'provide financial devolution to the Scottish Parliament' and, with it, greater 'responsibility'. Although he rejected 'Full Fiscal Freedom' as 'independence in disguise' Fraser said he 'strongly' supported the 'principles of financial devolution, where the Scottish Parliament is more responsible for the money it spends'. It was time for the party, he concluded, 'to be enthusiastic about the evolution of devolution' [Fraser, 2011].

At the same time Fraser advocated mirroring this greater autonomy in organisational terms by disbanding the Scottish Conservative Party and harking back to the 1912-65 period when the 'Scottish Unionist Party' (though he did not necessarily advocate that name) had existed alongside the UK Conservative and Unionist Party, without being part of it. This his rival for the leadership, Ruth Davidson, rejected out of hand, although she echoed Fraser in talking of a metaphorical 'line in the sand'. For Fraser this had been the party's recent election result, while for Davidson it was constitutional. The partial fiscal autonomy offered by the Westminster-initiated Scotland Bill, she argued, ought to be an end to talk of more powers. At this point, Davidson chose not to see the referendum as an opportunity, but referred to it in apocalyptic terms ('rip that union asunder') and promised to 'lead from the front' in opposition to it. 'I will make that positive case for the Union and together we will win as we have right on our side,' she said at her campaign launch. 'No half-way house, no second question – no march to fiscal autonomy. When the referendum is done, and Scotland in the Union has won the day, let that be an end to it.' In organisational terms, meanwhile, Davidson promised 'real change', 'change to the way we go about campaigning – structured funding, trained agents, supported candidates, genuine visibility, robust policy and a new media strategy which is not just cost effective but IS effective' [Davidson, 2011].

Davidson won the election, but her narrow victory coincided with significant shifts in the Conservative-led Coalition's referendum strategy. In January 2012 the Prime Minister chose to intervene, calling for a referendum that would be 'fair, legal and decisive' and offering to temporarily endow the Scottish Parliament with the powers to hold a ballot, subject to certain conditions. He also held out the possibility of a Westminster-initiated referendum should the SNP refuse to play ball, although that was never a realistic possibility given opposition from Liberal Democrats within the Coalition. This upped the ante considerably, but also caused problems for Ruth Davidson, particularly when, in a notable speech in February 2012, Cameron declared:

> This does not have to be the end of the road. When the referendum on independence is over, I am open to looking at how

the devolved settlement can be improved further. And yes, that does mean considering what further powers could be devolved. But that must be a question for after the referendum, when Scotland has made its choice about the fundamental question of independence or the United Kingdom. When Scotland has settled this question once and for all – and ended the uncertainty that I believe could damage and hold back Scotland's prospects and potential – then is the time for that issue [Cameron, 2012].

Davidson's 'line in the sand' had just been washed away, although it seemed the party did not intend to come up with a detailed scheme *before* the referendum took place. Making such a strategy credible in the eyes of voters, meanwhile, was made more difficult by a SNP narrative which invoked the ghost of another Old Etonian Conservative who had promised more powers for Scotland so long as it voted 'no'. 'The shadow of Sir Alec Douglas-Home I think is cast very large over this,' said Alex Salmond. 'What's the old saying: "fool me once, shame on you, fool me twice shame on me"? Scotland, I don't believe, will be fooled twice' [Currie, 2012].

Nevertheless, the party's referendum strategy was now firmly in the hands of the Westminster government, although it was often articulated via the Scottish leadership. Realising a referendum was inevitable, the Conservatives sought to have it held on terms it found acceptable, its priority being to prevent a second question on 'devo-max'. To that end it was therefore willing to cede ground to the Scottish Government on timing (Salmond was determined to hold the referendum in 2014-15) and the franchise (allowing 16- and 17-year-olds to vote). More widely the Conservative-led Coalition desired to appear 'reasonable', diligently avoiding any activity that could be depicted as 'anti-Scottish' by the SNP [Torrance, 2013].

Although regarded as a 'neutral figure' by Tory strategists (neither loved nor loathed in Scotland), the Prime Minister's involvement in the referendum campaign required careful handling. Labour was split when it came to campaigning alongside the Conservative leader (the shadow defence secretary Jim Murphy said he would not; the Scottish Labour leader Johann Lamont was more relaxed), while the prospect of a televised debate also posed a challenge. The SNP leader Alex Salmond repeatedly challenged David Cameron to a head-to-head joust before polling day, but after initial hesitation the Prime Minister demurred. 'This is not a debate between the SNP and the UK Conservative Party,' he said, 'it's a debate between people in Scotland.' Furthermore Cameron claimed a television debate was a 'diversion tactic' and observed that despite Salmond having spent most of his time 'telling me to butt out of Scotland's business, now he seems to want me to butt back in again' [Anonymous, 2013].

The 'Edinburgh Agreement' signed on 15 October 2012, meanwhile, delivered the Conservatives' main aim of committing the Scottish Government to a single referendum question, although Alex Salmond could also claim victory in having secured his preferred timing (the autumn of 2014) and a wider franchise. By this point the cross-party Better Together campaign had already been launched which, for obvious reasons was led by the former Labour Chancellor Alistair Darling rather than a senior Conservative or Coalition figure, although several Scottish Conservatives were involved behind the scenes (David McLetchie) and in its public events (both Ruth Davidson and Annabel Goldie were present at the Napier University launch).

Beyond Better Together, Conservative and Liberal Democrat ministers in London coordinated a series of 'Scotland Analysis' papers setting out the benefits of the Union, all of which were launched in Scotland by various Cabinet ministers, visitations the SNP claimed boosted the 'yes' vote, although there was little polling evidence to support this. At the March 2012 Scottish Tory conference in Troon, meanwhile, the party launched the 'Conservative Friends of the Union', a pro-UK campaign deliberately separate from the cross-party Better Together. Davidson shared a platform with UK Conservative co-chairwoman Baroness Warsi, the party's leader in the Lords, Lord Strathclyde, the then Welsh Secretary Cheryl Gillan, and former First Minister of Northern Ireland Lord Trimble, who between them represented the UK's four 'Home Nations'. The party appeared pleasantly surprised when 50,000 people donated almost £150,000 to the campaign within months of its launch [Cramb, 2012].

While it was true that support for independence was not confined to any one party there proved to be limited traction in Yes Scotland's attempt to appeal to a broad church. While it established two political sub-groups, 'Labour for Independence' and 'Liberal Democrats for Independence', it tellingly avoided making 'Conservatives for Independence' a third, even though several polls indicated that up to 5 per cent of Scottish Conservative voters might vote 'yes' in September 2014. There were at least two pro-independence Tories in the public eye: the historian and journalist Michael Fry (whose Scotfree2014 blog promoted independence from a libertarian perspective), and the Dutch financier Peter de Vink, who had been elected to Midlothian Council on a pro-independence Conservative ticket in May 2012.

Meanwhile, Scottish Conservative Party strategy gradually underwent another shift, with Ruth Davidson coming round to Murdo Fraser's analysis in relation to the constitution if not party organisation. One of her speeches extolled the virtues of US-style federalism, while by March 2013 she committed herself – with the Prime Minister's agreement – to greater fiscal autonomy for the Scottish Parliament. Davidson said:

> A parliament with little responsibility for raising the money it spends will never be properly accountable to the people of Scotland. It can never have the proper incentive to cut the size and cost of government, or to reduce tax bills. So that means in future a far greater share of the money spent by the Scottish Parliament should be raised by it. We will examine the mix of taxes best suited to achieving that goal, but the principle is clear. If you spend the public's money, then you must be accountable to the public both for how it is spent and how it is raised.

Davidson also explicitly linked her U-turn to the vote on independence. 'When the referendum comes in September next year,' she said. 'I don't want Scots to vote in fear of what the future might hold, but in the hope for what it can bring.' Working out detailed proposals was delegated to a commission chaired by Lord Strathclyde (no great fan, ironically, of devolution) while, acknowledging understandable 'suspicion' as to the party's motives, Davidson made a point of saying that the proposals would be included in the party's 2015 general election and 2016 Holyrood manifestos.

Importantly, Davidson's view of what ought to happen *after* the referendum was perhaps the clearest of the three Unionist parties, and went well beyond a commitment to greater powers. Once Scotland had 'rejected independence', she said, there needed 'to be a mechanism for establishing a consensus in Scotland on the shape of further devolution'. 'There will be no "empty chair" policy from the Scottish Conservatives', added Davidson, 'in any future gathering of Scotland's political and civic leaders to discuss our devolved settlement or future direction of our country.' Furthermore, she said the Scottish Conservatives would support Labour MP Douglas Alexander's 'helpful' proposal for a 'Scottish National Convention' to consider Scotland's 'social, economic and constitutional future' in the event of a 'no' vote.

> But fundamentally, we must find a means whereby we do not lurch from one commission to another, year after year; where the constitutional and commercial certainty we all crave is never reached. Where devolution is not viewed as a bilateral arrangement between Holyrood and Westminster, Cardiff Bay and Westminster or Stormont and Westminster. But a mechanism which reviews

devolution across – and within – our whole United Kingdom.

Above all both David Cameron and Ruth Davidson presented the independence referendum as an 'opportunity' for the Scottish Conservative Party. 'The referendum campaign must be a movement for us, as much as it is for the nationalists,' argued Davidson. 'This is not a big, nationwide by-election, it's our future. And there will be no second chance for those who believe in the UK. We must win next year, or lose forever' [Davidson, 2013].

Partisan motives, goals and behaviours

In opposing devolution between 1979 and 1997 the Scottish Conservative Party could hardly have been accused of doing so to protect its own interests. Re-evaluating this period and, even more importantly, the party's prospects, was an important sub-narrative of the referendum debate, and one that cast some light on the party's motivations. In standing for the leadership in the autumn of 2011, Murdo Fraser presented this in stark terms, telling his supporters that the Scottish Conservative Party, in 'its current state' was 'not fit for purpose'. Not only was it 'failing', he added, but it would 'never succeed in its current form' [Fraser, 2011]. Visiting Edinburgh in early 2012 the Prime Minister was less pessimistic but also realistic, telling journalists that he came to Scotland in a 'humble' spirit:

> I hope and wish that Scotland will vote to remain part of the United Kingdom. That is not because I want to dragoon Scotland into an arrangement that is in my interest or, frankly, in my party's interests. I know that the Conservative Party is not currently – how can I put this – Scotland's most influential political movement. I am often reminded that I have been more successful in helping to get pandas into the zoo than Conservative MPs elected in Scotland. So more than a little humility is called for when any contemporary Tory speaks in Scotland.

He also addressed the argument made by some Conservatives that an independent Scotland 'might make it easier for my Party to get a majority in Westminster'. 'But that does not interest me,' said Cameron. 'I am not here to make a case on behalf of my Party, its interests or its approach to office. I am here to stand up and speak out for what I believe in. I believe in the United Kingdom. I am a Unionist head, heart and soul' [Cameron, 2012]. A few weeks later he also rejected the idea that 'a small Conservative presence north of the border' was somehow 'inevitable'. 'This is our moment,' he added, 'if we are bold enough – to come back stronger' [Cameron, 2012b].

At the same time, the Prime Minister repeatedly emphasised to both Scottish and UK audiences how important he considered the referendum to be. 'There are many things I want this coalition to achieve, but what could matter more than saving our United Kingdom?' he told the 2012 UK Conservative Party conference in Birmingham. 'Let's say it: we're better together and we'll rise together – so let's fight that referendum with everything we've got' [Cameron, 2012c]. Ruth Davidson – who was given deliberate prominence at the 2013 Conservative Party conference in Manchester – was the most upbeat of the three, even amid growing discontent with her leadership in the course of 2013. 'When I was elected leader of the party', she told one journalist, 'I was pretty clear about the fact that things were going to have to change and you didn't reverse 19 years of stagnation and decline overnight' [Barnes, 2013]. 'We must stand up with confidence for what we believe,' she had urged during the 2012 UK Conservative Party conference. 'Because no one will believe in us if we don't believe in ourselves. The time for sack-cloth and ashes is over' [Davidson, 2012].

An important feature of Scottish Tory referendum strategy was a repudiation of its previous approach to constitutional reform. Murdo Fraser had already done this in the context of the debate surrounding greater powers, while Ruth Davidson argued that in playing 'a part in the writing of this new chapter', the Scottish Conservatives also had to 'turn over a new page'. She continued:

> With the benefit of hindsight, I believe we found ourselves on the wrong side of history in 1997. We fought on against the idea of a Scottish Parliament long after it became clear it was the settled will of the Scottish people. Our decision not to take part in the Scottish Constitutional Convention gave the impression that Scotland's constitutional future was not a matter of interest to us, beyond keeping Scotland in the UK. For many, the fact we were a lone voice saying 'no' in the referendum campaign simply underlined the impression we had no real faith in our own country. It made us look as if we lacked ambition for Scotland.

And although Davidson had been critical of Murdo Fraser's proposal to reconstitute the Scottish Conservative Party from scratch, she did echo his rhetoric in terms of how it conducted itself. 'We can talk to ourselves, as perhaps we have too often in the past,' she said. 'We can hold to the old ways and follow a path of slow decline. Or we can choose to do something about it.'

Choose to turn it around...Choose to build a modern Scottish Conservative party that speaks to the aspirations of mainstream Scotland. Which once again attracts the votes of people from every part of the country and every walk of life. I'm proud of our party's history, but we can't live in the past...If we are to meet the challenges of today, we can't endlessly refight the battles that have gone before. Scotland has moved on, and we have to move on too.

In backing greater autonomy for the Scottish Parliament, meanwhile, Davidson tried to do so in an explicitly Conservative manner, emphasising traditional Tory values like 'responsibility', cutting the 'size and cost of government' and reducing tax bills. She explained:

So that means in future a far greater share of the money spent by the Scottish Parliament should be raised by it. We will examine the mix of taxes best suited to achieving that goal, but the principle is clear...New powers over tax should mean one thing; tax rates being reduced and the burden of tax being lifted for every Scottish family...A Scottish Parliament that is more accountable to the people of Scotland...A Scottish government which can't hide from its responsibilities...A Scotland that stands on its own two feet but which doesn't stand alone in the world [Davidson, 2013].

As David Cameron argued in his speech to the 2012 Scottish Conservative Party conference, the 'challenge' was to 'reach out' to millions of people across Scotland who believed in 'some clear values', 'to reconnect their beliefs with ours'. This he said the party could do by 'driving three things home': that it was 'a distinctively Scottish party', 'a passionately patriotic party' and one whose 'values' chimed 'with the values of people all over Scotland' [Cameron, 2012b].

Davidson hoped that by stressing how 'essential' Conservatives were to winning the independence referendum and pressing ahead with organisational reforms the party would recover in electoral terms. There were twin targets in this respect, the 2015 general election and elections to the Scottish Parliament in 2016, although reports suggested the party's London HQ had given up counting on gains north of the border. 'Ruth Davidson has made a good start,' commented one Downing Street insider, 'but to rely on the Scottish Conservatives contributing anything substantial to the Westminster party after the next election would be a triumph of hope over experience' [Montgomerie, 2012].

The 2016 Holyrood election was taken more seriously, Davidson having introduced more rigorous selection procedures for candidates that would pit incumbent MSPs (including the party leader) up against newcomers, rather than virtually guaranteeing re-election for Conservatives predominantly elected via the Scottish Parliament's top-up list system. The process meant a third of Conservative councillors election in the 2012 local government elections had been new faces, a phenomenon the party hoped would be repeated in 2016.

The Scottish Conservatives' referendum discourse

In broad terms, the referendum campaign was dominated by two competing visions of what was best for the future of Scotland, 'independence' or maintaining the 'Union'. Although neither adequately captured what Yes Scotland and Better Together were actually proposing, these two 'nodal points' provided what was known in discourse theory as a 'chain of equivalence' [Laclau and Mouffe, 1985: 127-34], providing a context for each side to build a clear and understandable narrative around the nodal point they were seeking to promote. Conservative discourse was generally closer to Labour's, emphasising that Scotland in the UK was 'stronger together, better together', while devolution offered the 'best of both worlds', but did not go as far as that of the Liberal Democrats who talked about 'Home Rule', an attempt to position itself between two different camps.

The most important 'empty signifiers' [Laclau, 1996: 37] within Scottish Conservative discourse during the referendum campaign were 'Scotland' and 'Britain' (or 'Union'). This functioned within an overall narrative that since the beginning of the campaign sought to repeatedly emphasise the party's 'patriotism', as did the cross-party Better Together campaign (its website called it the 'patriotic all-party and non-party campaign for Scotland in the UK'). 'I am a Scot, and I am proud of my country,' declared Ruth Davidson in one speech.

> Like you, I want the best for Scotland; for us to be all we can be...To be a Scotland of freedom, opportunity, prosperity and fairness...And I understand what drives those who say they want independence for Scotland...Love of country...Patriotism...The hope and belief in a better future for all our people. I don't believe there is a single person in Scotland who does not understand those feelings; who does not share in that hope, belief and ambition for a better tomorrow. I know I do, and I know you do too. But no

political party – and no side in the constitutional debate – has a monopoly on patriotism [Davidson, 2013].

Scotland's future in the Union was therefore constructed around a chain of equivalent signifiers, the two most important being 'Scotland' and 'Britain/Union', and including 'freedom', 'opportunity', 'prosperity', 'fairness', and 'security'. According to this narrative, a 'patriotic' Scot could see the value in Scotland's 'place' in the Union and be no less patriotic. Elsewhere Davidson said Conservatives shared 'the nationalists' faith in Scotland's future' although their 'faith' was 'not blind to the facts' [Davidson, 2013b]. Similarly, David Cameron argued in 2012 that for 'too long' his party had 'let the SNP claim ownership of patriotism'.

The Saltire is the flag of a proud nation – not the symbol of one party. And that's the thing about the SNP. They've spread the idea that if you love your country, you have no choice but to go it alone, that believing in the Union is somehow treasonous. Do you know what one of their MSPs said? That leaders of the pro-United Kingdom parties were 'anti-Scottish'. This same SNP politician has also compared the United Kingdom to – I kid you not – an abusive relationship. What planet are these people on? This isn't an abusive relationship, it's a partnership – for liberty, security, prosperity [Cameron 2012b].

Discourse articulating the Union from the Conservatives also deployed metaphors of 'family' and 'partnership' of 'nations' to describe the 'relationship' between Scotland and the rest of the United Kingdom. This served to contest and subvert the Yes campaign's articulation of 'Scotland' around another chain of equivalences based on the nodal point of 'independence'. Questions of national identity were central to this discourse. Interestingly, the Prime Minister also acknowledged the complexities of what John P. Mackintosh called 'dual identity'. 'Not only can you can love Scotland and love the United Kingdom,' said Cameron, 'not only can you can drape yourself in the Saltire and the Union Jack, but you can be even prouder of your Scottish heritage than your British heritage – as many in Scotland are – and still believe that Scotland is better off in Britain' [Cameron 2012b].

Cameron and Davidson also repeatedly acknowledged the *possibility* of independence if not its *desirability*. The Prime Minister said he would never suggest 'Scotland could not make a go of being on its own'. 'Of course Scotland could govern itself,' he said. 'So could England. My point is that we do it so much better together' [Cameron, 2012a]. While Davidson, speaking as 'a proud Scot', rejected 'the notion we are somehow incapable of governing ourselves'. 'Of course we could,' she argued. 'But just because we could stand alone in the world, is not a reason for doing so'. Davidson also stressed Scotland's role in what she called 'a family of our four nations'. 'And we will fight today, tomorrow and every day between now and the referendum to defend Scotland's place in that family,' she said [Davidson, 2013].

One important strategy adopted by the Scottish Conservatives during the referendum was to counter claims from Yes Scotland that a No vote was a vote for the 'status quo', something that the Yes campaign has been highly critical of, and aspects of which it has focused heavily on. In particular, the Yes campaign has been keen to emphasise that a No vote would mean 'more of the same', particularly the effects of 'austerity', something it squarely associated with the 'Union'. To counter this, the Scottish Conservatives began to articulate a more nuanced position, as did Labour and the Liberal Democrats in different ways, a narrative that amounted to 'no, but'. First set out by the Prime Minister in his February 2012 speech in Edinburgh, this emphasised that voting 'no' in the referendum did not mean 'no change', an argument subsequently taken up by Ruth Davidson in speeches during 2013. 'So a "no" vote next year won't be a vote for "no change",' argued Davidson. 'Scotland wants change; needs change; and we are committed to helping deliver it' [Davidson, 2013]. Given the cynicism surrounding any Conservative pronouncements on devolution, Davidson also overcompensated in rhetorical terms. 'The breadth of our ambition must be much broader and the reforms we propose must go much deeper,' she said in August 2013, stressing that the referendum was an 'opportunity' to 'renew our place in the United Kingdom', to 'fashion a new constitutional settlement' and even 'to build a modern union for the next generation' [Davidson, 2013b]. This involved contesting and rearticulating some of the Yes campaign's key signifiers such as 'renewal', 'opportunity', 'modern', and the focus on future 'generations'. However, despite Davidson's rearticulation of the Party's position on the constitution, it did not help that polling showed Davidson to be the least popular of all the party leaders at Holyrood, a rating that did not significantly improve in two years at the helm.

Multi-level governance

The irony of devolution in 1999 was that it offered Conservatives, who had opposed both the creation of a Scottish Parliament and its proposed electoral system (proportional representation), the prospect of a political revival, as well as the possibility of carving out a political niche separate to that in Westminster, where it had been left without any representatives following the 1997 general election. In particular, it offered the opportunity to influence legislation (given that no party had an overall majority) and, perhaps, seek power via coalition with another party.

Table 1.1: Scottish Conservative Electoral Performance 1999-2005

Year	Level	Vote	Seats	Position
1999	Scottish Parliament	15.6%/15.3%	18	Opposition
1999	Local authority	13.5%	108	–
2001	UK Parliament	15.6%	1	Opposition
2003	Scottish Parliament	16.6%/15.5%	15+3=18	Opposition
2003	Local authority	15.1%	122	–
2005	UK Parliament	15.8%	1	Opposition

Given that the party had polled 17.5 per cent of the vote at its nadir in May 1997, the first two Scottish Parliament elections, at which the Scottish Conservatives polled 15.6 and 16.6 per cent of the vote respectively, it appeared devolution had not halted the party's electoral decline. But at the same time it won 18 seats in both, a respectable result in that it was more – in terms of votes and seats – than the Liberal Democrats (who formed a coalition Scottish Executive with Labour following each election). At the 2003 election, meanwhile, it won three constituency seats including Ayr, which it had gained at a by-election in 2000.

At Westminster the Scottish Conservative vote at first dipped (to 15.6 per cent in 2001) but then increased (albeit modestly) to 15.8 per cent in 2005 and 16.7 per cent in 2010, a figure not far removed from its 1997 showing. Perhaps surprisingly, the party showed its greatest improvement in local government elections. From 13.5 per cent of the vote and 108 councillors in 1999, it gained 15.1 per cent and 122 wards in 2003 and 15.6 per cent and 143 seats in 2007. Only in 2012 was this steady improvement checked, with the party polling just 13.3 per cent of the local government vote, enough to elect 115 council representatives.

Table 1.2: Scottish Conservative Electoral Performance 2007-2012

Year	Level	Vote	Seats	Position
2007	Scottish Parliament	16.6%/13.9%	13+4=17	Opposition
2007	Local authority	15.6%	143	–
2010	UK Parliament	16.7%	1	Coalition
2011	Scottish Parliament	13.9%/12.4%	12+3=15	Opposition
2012	Local authority	13.3%	115	–

In strategic terms, the party repeatedly struggled to find effective ways of campaigning in a devolved context, its perceived hostility towards the Scottish Parliament and the increasing weakness of its party organisation and grassroots support preventing significant progress. The 2010 general election campaign was a case in point, where – even with significant funds and attention from the Westminster party – a target of winning 12 seats produced just one, the same result it had achieved in 2005.

By contrast the Conservative Party in Wales, which had, since 1997, stressed its Welshness, generally accepted devolution (and campaigned for more of it) and worked hard to detoxify itself in the eyes of Welsh voters [Melding, 2012], had performed relatively well. Not only did the Welsh Conservative Party win the 2009 European Parliament elections in Wales, but in 2010 it gained eight MPs (having been left with none, like the Scottish Tories, in 1997), played a full part in campaigning for more powers in a March 2011 referendum and finally became the largest opposition party following the May 2011 Assembly elections. In other words, it had found a role for itself in post-1999 Wales, a constructive niche the Scottish party lacked.

At least in general elections, such as that in 2010, the party had a realistic chance of achieving power at a UK level, but in Holyrood elections its strategy of 2007-11 – becoming more 'relevant' via legislative co-operation with the minority Scottish Government – failed to produce the expected electoral dividend at the 2011 Holyrood election, when its vote was squeezed by a resurgent SNP vote. Internal critics of the SNP engagement strategy expressed concerns this had sent a signal to Tory-inclined voters that it was 'safe' to vote SNP. At the devolved level, the party also suffered from the actions of the Conservative-led Coalition government at Westminster. Even though much of the impact of planned austerity measures had yet to be felt (indeed the Treasury even agreed to delay its impact in Scotland), many well-worn narratives associated with a previous period of Conservative government (1979-97) resurfaced; indeed even when Baroness Thatcher passed away in 2013 the Scottish party still operated very much in her shadow, even though her effect on her party north of the border was generally misunderstood [Torrance, 2009]. Several commentators even suggested – unconvincingly – that an unintentional aspect of her legacy had been the 2014 independence referendum [Rawnsley, 2013].

Campaigning for the party's representatives to be elected to local councils, the Scottish Parliament, House of Commons or European Parliament was a known quantity, enabling Scottish Conservative activists to utilise traditional techniques (arguably the party dealt less deftly with PR elections), although the sociologist Alexander Smith argued that since 1997 Conservative activists cast to the geographical and institutional margins of Scotland had become 'banal' activists, burying themselves in paperwork and petty bureaucracy [Smith, 2011]. There were also fewer of them, with the party membership estimated – probably optimistically – to stand at around 10,000 members in late 2010 [Sanderson, 2010]. A referendum on independence, meanwhile, required a different sort of activism, one to which the SNP was much better suited. Although used to campaigning *against* devolution and, indirectly, against independence, Tory activists were not used to making arguments *for* the Union or, in the context of their leader's post-2013 strategy, *for* greater powers (especially when few of them agreed with that goal). This was the corollary of Michael Billig's 'banal nationalism', an unthinking Unionism that saw no need to justify itself.

Conclusion

The long run up to the independence referendum found the Scottish Conservative and Unionist Party in transition. Although the party had played a full role in the Scottish Parliament since 1999, Conservatives nevertheless continued to be associated with opposition to constitutional change, something the party finally confronted following poor results in both the 2010 and 2011 elections. And while a referendum on independence following the latter poll was unexpected (not least by the SNP), its prospect dovetailed with ongoing Scottish Tory thinking about its organisation, leadership and general strategy, all of which inevitably overlapped.

Its attempts to articulate a 'no, but' position between 2012 and referendum day in 2014 faced several challenges, not least internal opposition, grassroots apathy and SNP attempts to depict any Tory commitment to greater powers as a deception. Furthermore, in the electorate's mind the Scottish Conservatives had so long been associated with the 'Union' nodal point that getting voters to reimagine them as reforming devolutionists was inevitably difficult. Given the party's obvious weakness at the devolved level, further devolution could only be delivered by the party at Westminster, where the UK leadership increasingly emphasised its disinterest in electoral terms but also its willingness to be 'reasonable' and therefore constitutionally flexible. This dynamic was underlined by the virtual abandonment of any realistic strategy to rebuild the party's support north of the border.

Therefore despite significant shifts in party strategy towards the constitution, the prospect of increased Tory representation in Scotland following the 2015 UK general election or 2016 Holyrood election remained slim. Although between 2010 and 2015 the party was able to disguise its weakness via coalition with the Liberal Democrats (who had 11 Scottish MPs in contrast to one Conservative), a 2015-20 Tory majority – or indeed minority – government would present the Conservatives with a crisis of legitimacy in Scotland. Even before the 2015 election the SNP repeatedly stressed that this was a government Scotland had not 'voted for', a less potent version of their 1980s 'no mandate' argument.

But in stark contrast to previous periods of Conservative administration, after 2007 the party approached Scottish affairs with a very different mindset, acknowledging its weak position and expressing its willingness to consider devolving more power. This was increasingly reflected in its speeches (also analysed in this chapter), both David Cameron and Ruth Davidson emphasising that the party was determined not to repeat the mistakes of its past and had 'listened' to what the electorate wanted. In that context, the Scottish Conservatives were determined that 18 September 2014 represented an 'opportunity' for political recovery, rather than another nail in its electoral coffin, a chance to be – unlike in 1979 and 1997 – on the winning side of a constitutional referendum.

Bibliography

Allardyce, Jason [2009], 'Tory peer calls for independence poll' in *The Sunday Times (Scotland)*, Sunday, 23 August, 2009, online at: http://www.thesundaytimes.co.uk/sto/news/uk_news/article182848.ece

Arnott, Margaret and Macdonald, Catriona M. M. [2012], 'More than a Name: the Union and the Un-doing of Scottish Conservatism in the Twentieth Century' in Torrance, David (ed) [2012], *Whatever Happened to the Scottish Tories?*, Edinburgh, Edinburgh University Press.

Barnes, Eddie [2013], 'Ruth Davidson on her critics and Conservatism' in *Scotland on Sunday*, 2 June 2013, online at: http://www.scotsman.com/news/ruth-davidson-on-her-critics-and-conservatism-1-2951932

Cameron, David [2012a], *Speech in Edinburgh*, 16 February 2012, online at: https://www.gov.uk/government/speeches/transcript-pm-scotland-speech

Cameron, David [2012b], *Speech at Scottish Conservative Party conference*, 23 March 2012, online at: http://www.conservatives.com/News/Speeches/2012/03/David_Cameron_Scottish_Party_Conference.aspx

Cameron, David [2012c], *Speech at UK Conservative Party conference*,

10 October 2012, online at: http://www.conservatives.com/News/Speeches/2012/10/David_Cameron_Conference_2012.aspx

Conservative Party [1979], *manifesto*, London, Conservative Party, online at: http://www.conservative-party.net/manifestos/1979/1979-conservative-manifesto.shtml

Cramb, Auslan [2012], 'Campaign to stop Alex Salmond breaking up the UK attracts mass influx of funding and support' in *The Daily Telegraph*, 4 September 2012, online at: http://www.telegraph.co.uk/news/9519779/Campaign-to-stop-Alex-Salmond-breaking-up-the-UK-attracts-mass-influx-of-funding-and-support.html

Currie, Brian [2012], 'Salmond demands details on extra Holyrood powers' in *The Herald*, 17 February 2012, online at: http://www.heraldscotland.com/politics/political-news/salmond-demands-details-on-extra-holyrood-powers.1329447833

Davidson, Ruth [2011], 'Winning for Scotland' speech, 9 September 2011, online at: http://www.youtube.com/watch?v=99r68XFpMDU

Davidson, Ruth [2012], *Speech at UK Conservative Party conference*, 8 October 2012, online at: http://www.conservatives.com/News/Speeches/2012/10/Ruth_Davidson_Conference_2012.aspx

Davidson, Ruth [2013], 'Strengthening Scotland, Taking Scotland Forward' speech, 26 March 2013, online at: http://www.scottishconservatives.com/2013/03/strengthening-devolution-taking-scotland-forward/

Davidson, Ruth [2013b], 'A Union for the next generation' speech, 30 August 2013, online at: http://conservativefriendsoftheunion.com/2013/08/30/a-union-for-the-next-generation/

Fraser, Murdo [2011] 'A new party for Scotland' speech, 5 September 2011, online at: http://www.telegraph.co.uk/news/uknews/scotland/scottish-politics/8742143/Murdo-Fraser-reveals-plans-for-new-Scottish-Tory-party.html

Anonymous [2013], 'Cameron: I'm not having a "phoney" TV debate with Salmond', in *The Herald*, 4 April 2013, online at: http://www.heraldscotland.com/news/home-news/cameron-im-not-having-a-phoney-tv-debate-with-salmond.1365096853

Laclau, Ernesto and Chantal Mouffe [1985], *Hegemony & Socialist Strategy*, London, Verso.

Melding, David [2012], 'Refashioning Welsh Conservatism – a Lesson for Scotland?' in Torrance, David (ed) [2012] *Whatever Happened to the Scottish Tories?*, Edinburgh, Edinburgh University Press.

Montgomerie, Tim [2012], 'The Tory masterplan to win 36 seats from Labour and 14 from the Liberal Democrats' at Conservative Home, 3 May 2012, online at: http://conservativehome.blogs.com/majority_conservatism/2012/03/the-conservative-hq-plan-to-win-36-

seats-from-labour-and-14-from-the-liberal-democrats.html
Morton, Graeme [1999], *Unionist Nationalism: Governing Urban Scotland, 1830-60*, Edinburgh, Tuckwell Press.
Rawnsley, Andrew [2013], 'Thatcher: the unintended and paradoxical legacy of the lady in blue' in *The Observer*, 14 April 2013, online at: http://www.theguardian.com/commentisfree/2013/apr/14/thatchers-paradoxical-legacy
Sanderson, Lord [2010], *Building for Scotland: Strengthening the Scottish Conservatives*, Edinburgh, Scottish Conservative Party, online at: http://news.bbc.co.uk/1/shared/bsp/hi/pdfs/26_11_10_toryreport.pdf
Smith, Alexander [2011], *Devolution and the Scottish Conservatives: Banal activism, electioneering and the politics of irrelevance*, Manchester, Manchester University Press.
Torrance, David [2009], *'We in Scotland' – Thatcherism in a Cold Climate*, Edinburgh, Birlinn.
Torrance, David [2012], 'The Wilderness Years' in Torrance, David (ed) [2012] *Whatever Happened to the Scottish Tories?*, Edinburgh, Edinburgh University Press.
Torrance, David [2013], *The Battle for Britain: Scotland and the Independence Referendum*, London, Biteback Publishing.

6

The Scottish Liberal Democrats and the 2014 Independence Referendum

Malcolm Harvey

Introduction

The Scottish Liberal Democrats entered the Scottish independence referendum campaign in a position of both strength and of weakness; one which was unique among the unionist parties, but which had the potential to cause the party all manner of electoral difficulties. For while the party supported the Union and desired to maintain Scotland's position within the United Kingdom, the party adopted a position that was inherently different from their partners in the 'Better Together' campaign. As other chapters in this volume have indicated, the Conservatives and Labour sought to deliver a 'No' vote in the referendum to settle the constitutional question in favour of the Union, and to do so with limited change to the status quo. The Liberal Democrats, however, are federalists, and talked frequently of combining 'more powers' with 'more responsibilities' for the Scottish Parliament, delivering more 'Home Rule' for Scotland within a 'shared future' with the rest of the UK (Rennie, 2012a; 2012b). Articulating this vision of a 'strong Scotland' within a 'federal UK' was Scottish Liberal Democrat leader Willie Rennie, elected leader after a disastrous Scottish Parliament election for the party in May 2011, and Michael Moore, the Borders MP appointed Secretary of State for Scotland in the wake of the UK coalition government's election. Herein lay a major difficulty for the party in Scotland – for while they succeeded in achieving office (allowing the potential for policy influence and delivery) for the first time at UK level in 2010, governing with the Conservatives saw the party lose considerable electoral support in

Scotland, and their ability to influence the constitutional debate in the Scottish arena was considerably diminished. Nevertheless, with Moore as Secretary of State for Scotland, the Liberal Democrats were major players in the referendum campaign, though their own constitutional ambitions were largely absent from the debate. This chapter charts the evolution of the Scottish Liberal Democrats on the constitutional question, from their role in the Scottish Constitutional Convention and the Yes-Yes campaign in 1997 through coalition government in the Scottish Parliament from 1999-2007 to the recommendations of a series of commissions which helped influence the Scottish Liberal Democrats' constitutional positioning. It considers multi-level governance as 'a help and a hindrance' to the Liberal Democrats' constitutional ambitions, influencing the party's strategy on the constitutional issue but also limiting their opportunities to deliver upon their objectives. Finally, it considers the language which the party used to describe its constitutional objectives, arguing that the use of the phrase 'Home Rule' was designed to appeal to both supporters of independence and of the Union, being at once old-fashioned, familiar and safe yet at the same time radical, progressive and a bold change to the status quo. It is clear from this type of discourse that the Scottish Liberal Democrats are in a unique position in the constitutional debate, but a position which, despite their position in the UK coalition government, they were unlikely to be able to deliver upon.

The Evolution of Liberal Democrat Attitudes Towards Autonomy

The Liberals, the dominant party in nineteenth century Scotland, saw a decline in popularity in the early twentieth century while support for Labour was simultaneously on the rise (Keating, 2005:60). Though the split over Irish Home Rule in 1886 weakened the party significantly for a time with the emergence of the Liberal Unionists, Home Rule as a principle was one which the Liberal Party was to adhere to throughout the twentieth century, and one which would provide considerable impetus to the later party's constitutional objectives. As a much smaller party after the Second World War, the Liberals nevertheless had some impact upon the constitutional debate, no more so than in the 1970s when, with the Lib-Lab pact in operation, the party assisted in delivering the Scotland Act 1978 and the controversial devolution referendum in 1979. With limited numbers of Scottish MPs and members, the party's impact upon the campaign was small. Divisions within the party meant it did not affiliate to any of the cross-party groups but did establish its own internal organisation for the referendum and many local parties campaigned for a Yes vote. Party activists were involved in 41 per cent of local Yes groups and 68 per cent of local Liberal parties were active in the Yes campaign usually with leafleting, public meetings and transport to the polls [Bochel, Denver and Macartney 1982:48-52]. However, Liberal Party members made up a very small proportion of overall Yes activists and little finance was expended in the campaign [Bochel, Denver and Macartney 1982:52].

In the wake of the 1979 referendum defeat, devolutionists in Scotland formed an all-party Campaign for a Scottish Assembly, renewing efforts to bring devolution to Scotland. Two electoral victories for the Conservatives later, and a Scottish Constitutional Convention was established, in 1989, with participation from Labour and the Liberal Democrats, who sought to design a scheme for devolution (which the Scotland Act 1998 would eventually closely resemble). A key component of the scheme was a proportional electoral system for the parliament, with the additional member system the compromise accepted by both Labour and the Liberal Democrats (Bogdanor, 1998:197). The Liberal Democrats' long history of supporting Home Rule, made campaigning for a devolved Scottish Parliament a natural position for the newly established party to take. Nevertheless, working closely with Labour (and, indeed, the Scottish Trade Union Congress, and various other bodies) provoked some tensions within the Convention, none more so than the decision taken by Labour to put the devolution proposals to a referendum. The Liberal Democrats were furious at the lack of consultation involved in the decision, but, mindful of their desire to deliver devolution and the lesson from 1979 that unity was required if a successful outcome would be delivered, they – along with the SNP – joined Labour in supporting the cross-party Yes-Yes campaign for the referendum (Harvie and Jones, 2000:173-7). Political differences were put aside as the three quite distinct parties stood on a joint platform and campaigned successfully for a Scottish Parliament. Liberal Democrat activists were involved in local campaigning, with local parties running their own campaigns or cooperating with Scotland Forward. For example, 82 per cent of the local Liberal Democrat parties studied in the referendum were active in the Yes campaign, mostly in leafleting [Denver, Mitchell, Pattie and Bochel 1998:108]. There was very little canvassing done by the party and the campaign itself was seen to be much less intensive than the general election held in May 1997 [Denver, Mitchell, Pattie and Bochel 1998:112].

Given the proportional electoral system in place for the Scottish Parliament election, a majority for any party was never likely to materialise (though this sentiment was shattered by the SNP's majority in 2011). With Labour the largest party but lacking overall control in the newly-constituted parliament, they turned to their Convention colleagues, and the Scottish Liberal Democrats became junior partners in the first Scottish Executive from 1999-2003, with the parties renewing their agreement after the second Scottish election in 2003. This gave the party their first taste of governing, and though the junior partner, they were given several ministerial portfolios including party leader Jim Wallace taking on the Justice brief (as well as being named Deputy First Minister), Ross Finnie becoming Minister for Rural Affairs, and Nicol Stephen appointed as deputy Minister for Enterprise and Lifelong Learning. Though 1999-2003 could hardly be described as a smooth ride for the Scottish Executive, with 3 First Ministers in the first 3 years of devolution, this was not a result of tension within the coalition, which retained stability throughout the first term. Liberal Democrat ministers were responsible for the establishment of a Human Rights Commission for Scotland (Jim Wallace, in December 2001) and for the merging of the three water boards in Scotland to create Scottish Water (Ross Finnie, in March 2002) while the party itself made the abolition of upfront university tuition fees and the creation of legislation surrounding freedom of information priorities of the coalition agreement. Outside of those successes, their first taste of policy-making in office was limited to maintaining collective cabinet responsibility (Mitchell, 2003:132-3), though Roddin (2004) suggested that two-thirds of Scottish Executive policies started as Liberal Democrat initiatives (cited in Clark, 2012:104). However, to maintain stability, and continue the coalition into the second Scottish Parliamentary term (2003-2007), the Liberal Democrats' demands were greater. Here, the cost of doing business was electoral reform for local government – meaning implementation of their preferred electoral system, the Single Transferable Vote (STV) which would radically alter the make-up of Scotland's local authorities. Negotiations within the Labour Party were delicate, but in the end, pragmatism at Scottish Parliamentary level won over ambition at local level, and STV would be implemented prior to the following local government elections in 2007 (Scottish Labour/Scottish Liberal Democrats, 2003:46). Electoral reform was a long-standing Liberal Democrat policy, and that they secured their preferred proportional electoral system for local government elections was a clear commitment to local democracy and emphasised the party's instinct to allow decisions to be taken at the most appropriate level – evidence of their support for devolution, not only from the Westminster to Holyrood, but from Holyrood to the local level as well.

Support for devolution was evident from a further source too. The

Scottish Liberal Democrats, having spent all of the first two sessions of the Scottish Parliament as part of the governing coalition, believed the time was right to review the powers devolved to Holyrood. Lord Steel of Aikwood, the Parliament's first Presiding Officer, as well as a previous leader of the Liberals, was asked to chair a commission to consider the issue. The commission membership was varied, with a second member of the House of Lords, two MPs, three MSPs (including future leader Tavish Scott), four councillors and nine further members with varied links to the party joining Lord Steel to consider further devolution (Steel Commission, 2006:122). The Steel Commission reported in 2006, noting that the Liberal Democrats' 'support for Home Rule was, and continues to be, entrenched in [their] support for the principles of subsidiarity, democracy, accountability and power-sharing' (2006:6). Steel argued that 'despite the mutual benefits that can be clearly seen from the current union, there remains a clear argument for further reform to move towards a new modern settlement' (2006:54). The focus of his thinking with regards to reform was most particularly in the area of fiscal powers. At the Donald Dewar Memorial Lecture in 2003, Steel made this case clear: 'No self respecting Parliament should expect to exist permanently on 100% handouts determined by another Parliament, nor should it be responsible for massive public expenditure without any responsibility for raising revenue in a manner accountable to its electorate' (2006:54). To that end, the Steel Commission recommended a system of 'fiscal federalism'. Federalism had long been a Liberal Democrat policy, and Steel cited examples from Spain, Germany, Canada and Australia to emphasize how such a system might work. Rejecting 'full fiscal autonomy' within the UK, Steel recommended that the Scottish Parliament be given the powers to raise as much of its own spending as possible. This included devolving some economic levers in business regulation and taxation, and providing some borrowing powers for the parliament. Steel's reasoning was that 'greater accountability is not an abstract matter, but a principle of good and effective government,' (2006:55) and that greater accountability in terms of spending could only be achieved by allowing the parliament powers over revenue raising as well. Steel also wanted to overcome the 'anomalies' which existed in the Scotland Act 1998 by devolving to the Scottish Parliament powers over the electoral system and the rules and standing orders of the Scottish Parliament itself; the remaining reserved transport issues and medical contracts (given the majority of powers in these areas had already been devolved); further powers over energy policy (for example, in the fields of nuclear and renewable energy, which remained partially reserved); and to create an entirely separate Scottish civil service (2006:70-1).

However, with the SNP minority government replacing the Labour-Liberal Democrat coalition after the 2007 election, the Liberal Democrats' ability to take forward Lord Steel's recommendations diminished: not least as the party refused to enter coalition talks with the SNP after the election. The SNP's electoral success and creation of a minority government did push forward constitutional debate though. The new government launched a National Conversation on constitutional reform, using the process to discuss and promote independence and other constitutional options short of independence [Harvey and Lynch 2012]. In an attempt to regain the initiative on the constitutional issue, the Conservatives, Labour and Liberal Democrats joined together and established the Commission on Scottish Devolution in 2008 (known as the Calman Commission). Much like the Liberal Democrats' Steel Commission, Calman's report in 2009 sought to consider how the devolution settlement might be altered while maintaining Scotland's place within the United Kingdom. The task of the Calman Commission was:

> To review the provisions of the Scotland Act 1998 in the light of experience and to recommend any changes to the present constitutional arrangements that would enable the Scottish Parliament to serve the people of Scotland better, improve the financial accountability of the Scottish Parliament, and continue to secure the position of Scotland within the United Kingdom (Commission on Scottish Devolution, 2009).

The Calman process brought proposals to devolve some small tax and policy powers, introduce an income tax-substitution scheme to fund the Scottish Parliament, as well as giving Holyrood the ability to borrow money to fund infrastructure [Commission on Scottish Devolution 2009]. Most of these powers were devolved to Scotland through the Scotland Act 2012. While the Liberal Democrats were involved in the Calman process, with 2 representatives on the Commission, they did not instigate this commission, nor were they happy with the interim report the Commission served up, fearing that it lacked the necessary changes that the devolution settlement required (Wallace, 2008). What Calman proposed was much less radical than the Steel Commission with no link to UK devolution reforms. However, by the time the final report found its way into legislation, the Liberal Democrats were in coalition with the Conservatives and the party was responsible for negotiating and legislating for Calman through the Scotland Office and Secretary of State Michael Moore as part of the coalition deal. Nevertheless, the Calman Commission, and the Scotland Act it spawned, did not provide the radical – fiscal and federal – constitutional changes the Scottish Liberal Democrats sought.

After two elections, the 2010 UK election and the 2011 Scottish election, with widely different outcomes for the party (considered in more detail below), new Scottish leader Willie Rennie appointed former Liberal Democrat leader Menzies Campbell to lead a further commission to consider the Scottish Liberal Democrat position with regards to the upcoming Scottish independence referendum. The Campbell Commission reported in 2012, arguing for a 'radical' allocation of tax and borrowing powers to Holyrood, allowing the Scottish Parliament to raise around two thirds of its own revenue (The Home Rule and Community Commission of the Scottish Liberal Democrats, 2012:10). The Campbell Commission's report built upon the Steel Commission's recommendations, setting out a clear explanation of fiscal federalism, while also reaffirming that the Scottish Liberal Democrats were 'federalists, in favour of home rule for Scotland within a reformed, federal UK' (2012:8). Campbell argued that the referendum was an opportunity for the Liberal Democrats to build a federal project, stating that 'a rejection of independence will enable Scotland to continue down the track towards a modern, pluralist and federal relationship with the other parts of the United Kingdom' (2012:19). Thus, the Scottish Liberal Democrats – unlike their Unionist colleagues Labour and the Conservatives in the Better Together campaign – were actively seeking radical constitutional change. However, that change remained predicated on Scotland's continued future within the UK, meaning that the party remained committed to the Union and Scotland's place within it – and actively campaigned for a 'No' vote in the independence referendum. Alongside the Campbell Commission recommendations were further Liberal Democrat initiatives, such as an increased movement towards localism (particularly with regards to policing and health policies, which had featured heavily in the party's 2011 election manifesto) as well as the suggestion from Michael Moore that Scotland's islands would require more autonomy whatever the outcome of the independence referendum. Both suggestions leaned heavily on the principle of subsidiarity.

The Scottish Liberal Democrats were also semi-officially engaged with the *Devo-Plus* campaign, run by their former MSP Jeremy Purvis [later nominated by the party to the House of Lords]. The group was guided by three MSPs – Tavish Scott (Liberal Democrat), Alex Fergusson (Conservative) and Duncan McNeil (Labour). This was intended to provide the group with a cross-party basis for their proposals, which drew heavily on the recommendations of both the Steel and Campbell commissions. The proposals set out a means of implanting Steel's suggestion that the Scottish Parliament should have control over its own revenue by establishing three clear brackets for taxation: those which would be fully devolved, fully reserved or shared between the two institutions. Specifically, *Devo Plus* called for VAT and National Insurance to continue to be reserved while Income Tax and Corporation Tax would be shared more equally between the two levels (Devo Plus, 2012:5), with further transfers of tax powers outlined in the proposals over time – including oil revenues.

Party Strategy for the Referendum

While the role of Scottish Liberal Democrat activists in the referendum campaign was limited due to lack of resources, the strategy of the party hierarchy was quite clear. For while multi-level governance had provided electoral difficulties for the party, entering office at UK level provided the party with an opportunity to make progress towards their policy goals. In Müller and Strøm's terminology, the party prioritised office success over policy (1999:5) as a means of showing voters that the party was a legitimate contender for government office. This focus on office success allowed the party to secure key cabinet appointments, with the trade-off being that Conservative concessions on policy were limited. Given the Conservatives' lack of electoral success in Scotland (with only one MP – David Mundell) it made sense for David Cameron to appoint a Scottish Liberal Democrat as Secretary of State for Scotland. Danny Alexander was briefly appointed, before he was required to replace David Laws as Chief Secretary to the Treasury, and Michael Moore subsequently replaced him. Michael Moore's early role was to oversee the recommendations of the Calman Commission, and to pilot the subsequent legislation through the UK Parliament. When the bill was launched on 30 November 2010, Moore argued that the bill was 'the culmination of work by three Scottish political parties, numerous impartial experts, two successive UK Governments and the two Parliaments in London and Edinburgh' (Scotland Office, 2010). At that stage, the bill included devolution of powers over air weapons, drink-drive limits and national speed limits (as recommended by the Calman Commission), as well as tax powers accounting for 35% of the Scottish budget. Until 2011, while the SNP remained a minority government at Holyrood, Moore's job in piloting the legislation was relatively straightforward, for even though the bill was to be considered by committees at both the UK and Scottish parliaments (the first time the Scottish Parliament had been granted status as a co-legislature), the latter's committee (again, until 2011) contained an opposition majority, meaning any attempts made by the SNP to amend the legislation could come to naught. However, after the SNP was returned as a majority government after the 2011 election, Moore's job became more problematic and piloting the bill a more delicate operation, especially since the SNP now had a majority on each of the Scottish Parliament's committees and an effective veto power over the Scotland bill. Prior to the election, David Cameron had tried – and largely succeeded – in portraying Moore as on the same level as First Minister Alex Salmond, thereby enhancing the importance of the role of the Secretary of State for Scotland while at the same time attempting to diminish the role of the First Minister. This meant that any negotiations on the Scotland Bill (and, indeed, discussions held on the prospect of a referendum) between the Scottish Government and the UK Government were conducted through Michael Moore, giving the Scottish Liberal Democrats a measure of control over the process at a critical time. Not only did Moore face a SNP government dedicated to holding an independence referendum but he also faced competition from within the UK government for control of the referendum issue from numerous senior actors. Moore's response to these challenges was to seek to seize control of the political agenda by launching a consultation process on the independence referendum in January 2012.

The UK Government's proposals on the Scottish constitutional issue – a white paper titled *Scotland's Constitutional Future*, and a two month consultation period between January and March 2012 – were somewhat upstaged by Alex Salmond's announcement of the Scottish Government's consultation for the referendum live on STV's evening news programme. However, while the announcement was undoubtedly a political coup for the SNP, Moore and the UK Government sought to regain the initiative, particularly on process, with the white paper seeking to provide clarity on what they described as a 'legal, fair and decisive' referendum (HM Government, 2012). The UK Government's Advocate General, former Scottish Liberal Democrat leader Jim Wallace, focused particularly on the legality of the referendum issue, noting that a Section 30 order would be required to provide the Scottish Parliament with the legislative capability to deliver a referendum.

In October 2012, negotiations between the UK and Scottish Governments were concluded, and a document co-authored by Michael Moore (for the UK Government), Bruce Crawford and Nicola Sturgeon (for the Scottish Government) was made public. The *Agreement between the United Kingdom Government and the Scottish Government on a referendum on independence for Scotland* (which became known as the Edinburgh Agreement) was signed by Prime Minister David Cameron and Secretary of State for Scotland Michael Moore on behalf of the UK Government, and by First Minister Alex Salmond and Deputy First Minister Nicola Sturgeon for the Scottish Government on 15 October 2012. The agreement set out the process that should be followed in the upcoming legislation for the referendum. The UK Government felt it had fulfilled its objectives in the negotiation as the agreement required the referendum to be a single question (which ruled out having the option of 'devo-max' on the ballot paper), that a Section 30 order would require to be legislated for first, and that the referendum should take place before the end of 2014. The Scottish Government on the other hand, claimed victories on the fact that they would maintain control of the referendum legislation (it would be legislated for by the Scottish Parliament) and that the franchise would, for the first time, be extended to allow 16 and 17 year olds to vote in the referendum (HM Government/Scottish Government, 2012). Thus both sides could be reasonably happy with the outcome of the negotiations, though the fact that Prime Minister David Cameron travelled to Edinburgh to sign the agreement certainly gave the Scottish Government a substantial media coup.

Nevertheless, for the Scottish Liberal Democrats – particularly those involved closely with the UK coalition government – the Edinburgh Agreement proved something of a double-edged sword. On the one hand, the document established clear criteria for the referendum and set-out the process in detail, ensuring that the legislation could be passed by the Scottish Parliament without the threat of a legal challenge (an issue which Jim Wallace had been particularly exercised about). The clarity brought to the process by the agreement was welcome, and also allowed Moore to provide some Liberal Democrat thinking into the process. On the other hand, the agreement did not specify any further devolution of power should a 'No' vote prevail in the referendum itself. Thus, whilst the Liberal Democrats succeeded to an extent in influencing the outcomes of the Edinburgh Agreement, those outcomes were not consistent with their own objectives. The party's strategy post-Edinburgh Agreement was to join with Labour and the Conservatives in the Better Together organisation and campaign for a 'No' vote in the referendum in the hope that a negative outcome in this referendum would lead to a further devolution of powers to the Scottish Parliament (and, indeed, dramatic changes to the constitution of the entire UK) in the mould of fiscal federalism. That the party would remain in office at UK level until after the referendum, and could thus attempt to influence UK Government policy on the constitution, was seen as a benefit to this strategy.

Partisan Motives, Goals and Behaviours

Having worked with Labour in the Scottish Constitutional Convention to draw up blueprints for a Scottish Parliament, the 1997 devolution referendum in Scotland gave the Scottish Liberal Democrats a clear opportunity to complete the process, and the party joined the Yes-Yes campaign, along with Labour and the SNP. Campaigning in this referendum was a complex composition of cross-party co-operation (through the campaign body Scotland Forward) and the individual parties themselves campaigning locally and nationally on their own. For the Liberal Democrats – firm proponents of the principle of subsidiarity – devolution was a principle worth supporting, and the party were motivated to campaign for the principle. As an added bonus, the semi-proportional electoral system which was to be adopted for the parliament would provide the party with better representation in Scotland than the majoritarian first-past-the-post (FPTP) system of elections to the UK Parliament, providing an electoral motive to support the principle. Contrast this with the party's campaigning at the 2011 UK-wide referendum on the Alternative Vote (AV) electoral system. While electoral reform has been a long-term Liberal Democrat policy objective, AV was not their preferred choice. While it was preferable to the FPTP electoral system, it was hard for activists to get excited about an electoral system which was a marginal improvement on the status quo. The public too, was cynical about the change, and with Liberal Democrat activists indifferent about AV, convincing the electorate became a more difficult prospect. In short, while the system would have benefitted the party electorally, it was not seen as a significant improvement, thus activists lacked the motivation to campaign for it. It was hard not to see some parallels here with the independence referendum.

There were two clear facets to Scottish Liberal Democrat campaigning in the referendum. The first of those was the cross-party campaign for a 'No' vote, Better Together, which featured Labour, the Conservatives and the Liberal Democrats. As in 1997, this meant three parties combined to work together under one banner. Similar to 1997 was the fact that all three parties were pulling in slightly different directions, and indeed, were motivated by different factors. The Conservatives began with their Scottish leader's 'line in the sand' against more devolution which was washed away by the UK leader, David Cameron, with the promise to consider more devolved powers in the event of a 'No' vote. Labour, meanwhile, produced an interim review of its policy on devolution but remained divided between

MPs and MSPs on future devolution. The Scottish Liberal Democrats though, actively supported a 'No' vote with the explicit objective of encouraging further devolution short of independence. That each of the three parties desired distinctly different outcomes from a straight Yes-No referendum added an interesting dynamic to the referendum and created an inherent tension within the Better Together campaign itself: to add to the political tensions over Westminster party competition and the UK government. Equally, the division of labour between party activists within the Better Together campaign was problematic for the unity of the campaign, with individual party interests – and, indeed, fundamental differences on the constitutional issue – able to undermine the potential for the campaign's success. While each of the three was campaigning for the same short-term outcome (a 'No' vote), medium-to-long term objectives were very different, both on the constitutional issue itself and from a partisan, electoral perspective.

This led to the second facet of Liberal Democrat campaigning at the referendum: the individual party campaigning at local level. While the Better Together campaign provided a national focal point for a 'No' vote, with national campaign weekends and media events, parties themselves continued to campaign on an individual basis. And given the lack of motivation to campaign on the referendum issue itself, in its early stages the focus of local party campaigning was less on the referendum and more on the future prospects of success for their party in constituencies. On the ground, this meant targeting known areas of strength at constituency and ward levels, with the focus of campaigning the 2015 UK General Election rather than the referendum. And, for the Liberal Democrats this created a fairly substantial challenge given the party's electoral losses in Scotland in 2011 and 2012. For example, at the UK general election in 2010, the party targeted marginal seats like Aberdeen South, Edinburgh North and Leith and Edinburgh South in addition to holding the seats it had won in 2005. However, there was no prospect of this strategy being repeated in 2015. Rather, the party was focused on defending existing seats through policy differentiation in the coalition, claiming policy gains, promoting its role in restraining its Conservative partners and emphasising the constituency-service role of incumbent MPs.

This defensive strategy was made easier by the lack of boundary changes in advance of the 2015 election. Specifically, the Liberal Democrats were targeting four Scottish constituencies for the UK election – Argyll and Bute, East Dunbartonshire, Edinburgh West, and West Aberdeenshire and Kincardine – where the party had most to fear from their role in coalition with the Conservatives. Each of these seats was lost to the SNP at the 2011 Scottish election and has vulnerabilities to both Labour and the SNP challenges in 2015. This reality created interesting dynamics and dilemmas on the ground during the referendum campaign – to what extent should party activists combine with Labour activists in Edinburgh West or East Dunbartonshire who were working to remove the party's MP? The question tapped into the primary motivations of the party on the ground – is it the party or the referendum vote? For Liberal Democrat party activists there was the post-coalition challenge of improving the ailing fortunes of the party at the forthcoming elections following serious reverses after 2010. This highlighted a clear difficulty for the Better Together camp – how to maintain the unity of three parties who agree on the benefits of the Union (though not on their constitutional preferences) while the parties themselves still had their own electoral interests at heart. In the early stages of the referendum campaign – when opinion polls suggested that a 'No' vote was comfortably ahead – this was not that problematic but as the referendum approached, and with the likelihood that the polls would tighten, these tensions were more problematic. Scottish Labour established 'United with Labour', in part to give the party some distance from their Conservative and Liberal Democrat colleagues who were part of the UK Government and, in particular, to distance themselves from the UK Government's so-called 'Bedroom Tax'. With the Liberal Democrats campaigning on an individual basis (and focused more upon the upcoming 2015 election), and with the electoral competition and, more particularly, the ideological differences between the parties coming to the fore on issues such as the Bedroom Tax, the impact upon Better Together was that the campaign became less cohesive – an issue which was largely avoided by the 1997 cross-party Yes-Yes campaign which occurred after the general election, rather than months before it when the UK parties are in election-mode.

The Scottish Liberal Democrats' Referendum Discourse

The independence referendum campaign was characterised by conflict over two competing notions of the best future for Scotland: striking out alone as an independent sovereign state (on the side of Yes Scotland) or continuing with the 300-year-old Union (on the side of Better Together). Within that context, it is of interest to note that the contest was not solely about winning over voters but also about winning the battle to define concepts. In discourse analysis, these 'empty signifiers' are a clear indication of the ground upon which a party is attempting to win on an issue, and to establish their definition of a concept as the prevailing understanding of it. Arranging these empty signifiers around a nodal point (in this context, 'independence' or 'the Union') provides what is known in discourse theory as a 'chain of equivalence' (Laclau and Mouffe, 1985:127-34). Chains of equivalence provide a context for the contested concepts and assist actors in building a clear and understandable narrative around the nodal point which they are seeking to promote. The Scottish Liberal Democrat discourse on the constitutional question was interesting in its distinctiveness from the Better Together campaign, as this section will demonstrate.

The fundamental aspects of the referendum campaign – that is, the two cross-party campaigns – focused on two distinct chains of equivalence. Yes Scotland focused on providing a positive discourse around the nodal point of independence while at the same time seeking to associate a negative chain of equivalence around the second nodal point, the Union. Better Together, naturally, focused upon the opposite. The Scottish Liberal Democrats were distinctive because they fell between the two camps – as previously considered, they do not want independence for Scotland, but nor is the status quo of an unaltered UK constitution appealing to the party. Thus, while the party competed on the same field as Better Together colleagues in building a positive discourse around the nodal point of the Union, they did not engage quite so much with the negative discourse around the concept of independence. Rather, the Scottish Liberal Democrats attempted to create a third nodal point around the concept of 'Home Rule for Scotland'. This was apparent through the promotion of policies around localism – the local income tax, opposition to the centralisation of Scotland's policing and a focus on local healthcare – and in calls for greater autonomy for the island councils of Orkney, Shetland and Comhairle nan Eilean Siar (Scottish Liberal Democrats, 2011:71; Scott and McArthur 2012).

In doing so, the party borrowed empty signifiers associated with both Yes Scotland's positive chains of equivalence around independence and Better Together's positive chains of equivalence around the Union. Those associated with independence included: 'Scotland', 'more powers', 'more responsibilities', 'strong Scotland', 'fair society', 'strong economy' and 'parliament'. Those associated with the Union included: 'United Kingdom', 'consensus', 'partnership', 'devolution', 'Home Rule', 'fiscal federalism', 'federal UK', 'strong Scotland' and 'shared future'. Combined, these empty signifiers gave an almost neutral association with both nodal points of independence and the Union, noting the strengths of each position rather than providing any kind of negative consideration to either. And this was clearly where the Liberal Democrats were attempting to position themselves on the constitutional question – that neither independence nor the Union as it was presently constructed could provide the best for Scotland, and that their preferred option, fiscal federalism and Home Rule for Scotland within the context of a federal UK constitution, would actually provide the 'best of both worlds'.

Willie Rennie's comments in the preface to the Campbell Commission report provide evidence of this discursive strategy: 'Home rule for Scotland could work well, but would be even better if it were part of a move towards a federal United Kingdom, where every part of the United Kingdom could have similar levels of responsibility.' (The Home Rule and Community Commission of the Scottish Liberal Democrats, 2012:3). Here he was clear not to be negative about the nodal point of independence, but to emphasise the positives of the Union and stress the key difference between the Liberal Democrats and their Better Together campaign fellows – the concept of federalism. His conference speeches centred on similar themes, telling the Scottish Liberal Democrat conference in March 2012 that:

> We should set out the potential for Scotland, a powerful force within the United Kingdom, with domestic control through home rule – that's a good reason to reject independence… It may be that – after the No vote – the SNP can survive the ending of their dream. We and they could well be able to work together afterwards to shape a home rule future for Scotland. (Rennie, 2012a)

However, Rennie was at pains to point out that it was the Liberal Democrats alone who were offering this distinctive constitutional position, empathising the history of Home Rule within the party:

> But be in no doubt. Those three other parties might say they want home rule but they are only taking their first, hesitant, infant steps. We will need to be the ones who bring people together and bring people along. We will be the guarantors of change. Liberal Democrats have wanted home rule for a hundred years… [A] Scotland with the powers to run our home affairs but proud to share the wins and share the risks with the United Kingdom family of nations. (Rennie, 2012a)

Indeed, even when he was speaking to the federal party's conference in September 2012, Rennie was keen to establish his Scottish party's credentials as federalists and Home-Rulers:

> We don't want Scotland to break from the rest of the UK but we do want to change it; to deliver home rule with more powers

so that Scotland can determine its own destiny on the domestic agenda whilst sharing the risks and rewards with the rest of the UK. (Rennie, 2012b)

We can view this as clear evidence that the Scottish Liberal Democrat leader wanted to establish a clear and distinct constitutional position for the party which was not limited by the polarised referendum debate. Here it was clear that the Scottish Liberal Democrats were attempting to create a third pole. This was significant for the referendum campaign as, although their constitutional preference did not form part of the referendum question, the Scottish Liberal Democrats were attempting to ensure that it was part of the constitutional debate. Were the Scottish electorate to reject independence in 2014, then the work undertaken to build the alternative nodal point 'Home Rule' could be a key part of the subsequent constitutional debate. The Scottish Liberal Democrats' discursive strategy thus had a two-fold purpose. Firstly, the primary objective was to provide an alternative to the Yes-No debate upon which the referendum was fought, and to encourage a 'No' vote on the basis that their constitutional policy would suit Scotland better than either of the two options that were on offer in the referendum. Secondly, the objective was to build up this alternative to the point that, in the event of a 'No' vote, the public were aware that such an option existed and were positive about the prospects for its success [leading to increased support for the Liberal Democrats].

Multi-Level Governance And The Independence Referendum

The establishment of devolved institutions in Scotland and Wales in 1999 was a dramatic alteration to the UK's unwritten constitution, and it brought a whole new manner of political competition. Parties could now be in opposition at UK level while governing in devolved institutions and vice versa. Added to the pre-existing local authorities, devolution provided parties with much more to consider in the way of electoral strategies, potential governing coalitions and relationships with other parties. Unlike the Conservatives and Labour, the Scottish Liberal Democrats are largely autonomous of their partners in the rest of the UK, with a level of policy and organisational autonomy within the federated framework of the party (Keating, 2005:60; Lynch, 1998:24-5). This allows the party to retain distinct policy objectives in Scotland, but, with unified symbols and electoral rhetoric, as well as a strategy which does not differ markedly, the actions of the federal party do impact upon the fortunes of the Scottish party.

Table 1.1: Scottish Liberal Democrat Electoral Performance 1999-2005

Year	Level	Vote	Seats	Position
1999	Scottish Parliament	14.1%/ 12.4%	12/ 5 = 17	Coalition
1999	Local authority	12.7%	156	–
2001	UK Parliament	16.4%	10	Opposition
2003	Scottish Parliament	15.3%/ 11.8%	13/ 4 = 17	Coalition
2003	Local authority	14.5%	175	–
2005	UK Parliament	22.6%	11	Opposition

For the Scottish Liberal Democrats, the first two terms of the Scottish Parliament provided a very positive experience of multi-level governance. Successive UK elections in the 1990s and early 2000s had left the federal party as a clear third party in UK politics while, with 10 seats in Scotland, the party was firmly established as the second largest (in terms of parliamentary seats held) behind Labour. Winning 17 seats in the Scottish Parliament in both 1999 and 2003 led to the party entering coalition government in Scotland. Add in to the mix that the Welsh Liberal Democrats had entered a coalition, also with Labour, in the National Assembly for Wales between 2000 and 2003 (albeit with a much smaller body of representatives), multi-level governance looked to be utterly unchallenging to the party.

Table 1.2: Scottish Liberal Democrat Electoral Performance 2007-2012

Year	Level	Vote	Seats	Position
2007	Scottish Parliament	16.2%/11.3%	11/ 5 = 16	Opposition
2007	Local authority	12.7%	166	–
2010	UK Parliament	18.9%	11	Coalition
2011	Scottish Parliament	7.9%/5.3%	2/ 3 = 5	Opposition
2012	Local authority	6.6%	71	–

The Liberal Democrats at all levels – UK, devolved and local authority – appeared to be united and successful. There was little internal conflict between the different levels and the part functioned well both as a governing party in the devolved legislatures and as an opposition party at Westminster (Clark, 2012:103). Even after the Welsh Liberal Democrats lost their coalition status in 2003 and the Scottish Liberal

Democrats lost theirs in 2007, multi-level governance did not provide any serious issues for the party. If anything, being in opposition at all levels helped the party to retain a coherent message – meaning that, with the party no longer in government at any level, there was no danger of inconsistency in message.

However, this situation changed fundamentally after the 2010 UK General Election resulted in a hung parliament. Entering into a coalition with the Conservative Party was never going to be the most popular of decisions and the Liberal Democrats entered government at UK level for the first time. The decision to cross the threshold from opposition into government is not be taken lightly by any party, not least because there are a number of important factors which may influence their decision. For Müller and Strøm these goals can be understood with reference to three concepts: policy, office and votes (1999:5). For the UK Liberal Democrats, this was an opportunity to enter office at this level for the first time in an effort to counteract the widespread belief among voters that the party would never form the UK government (Clark, 2012:103). Given their entry into government in the middle of a global recession and the austerity measures which followed, voters blamed the Liberal Democrats for a number of unpopular initiatives, including the raising of university tuition fees in England and Wales and the 'Bedroom Tax'. While estimates of coalition policy commitments suggest that while there were notable 'wins' for the Liberal Democrats, these were 'at best mixed wins' with several policy objectives severely watered down (Clark, 2012:105). Even in areas where a clear Liberal Democrat policy was met – such as raising the tax threshold – there was only a partial victory, given the length of time it took to phase in the policy. In short, governing in coalition with the Conservatives led to a considerable public backlash against the party.

This was no truer than in Scotland. While David Cameron's Conservatives had performed better in 2010 in the rest of the UK than they had at any election since 1992, the party had only returned 1 MP in Scotland, leaving questions once again over the legitimacy of their mandate to govern Scotland. The legitimacy was to be provided by the Liberal Democrats, who had 11 Scottish MPs in 2010 – including two members of the cabinet in Danny Alexander, the Chief Secretary to the Treasury and Michael Moore, the Secretary of State for Scotland. The Scottish Liberal Democrats were cast as the 'human shields' for the coalition in Scotland and became scapegoats for the some of the UK coalition's more unpopular policies through their alliance with the 'toxic' Conservatives. And this is where multi-level governance started to cause the Liberal Democrats big problems.

The Scottish Parliament election of 2011 saw the Liberal Democrats lose 8% of their constituency vote and 6% of their regional vote. This resulted in 11 fewer MSPs, reducing the party from 16 seats to just five, and wiping out all their constituencies on the mainland. Only Tavish Scott (Shetland) and Liam McArthur (Orkney) were returned as constituency MSPs. Willie Rennie – who lost his Westminster by-election gain in 2010 – entered the Scottish Parliament as one of three regional list MSPs, and subsequently replaced Tavish Scott as the party leader. However, worse was to follow in the 2012 local authority elections. The Scottish Liberal Democrat first preference vote was halved and the party lost 95 councillors as a result. In five years, the collective representation of the party in Scotland had dropped from 193 MPs, MSPs and councillors in 2007 to 87 in 2012. This had a direct impact on the ability of the party to campaign at all levels in significant ways, with implications for its referendum campaigning and performance at the European election of 2014, UK election of 2015 and Scottish election of 2016.

The Liberal Democrat electoral model across Britain was built upon localism and pavement politics: intensive use of the Focus leaflets and campaigning on local issues to develop a profile in council wards that would build up into electoral success and parliamentary representation [Russell and Fieldhouse 2004]. However, a number of organisational difficulties and electoral failures after 2010 began to undermine a campaigning model built on activism and incumbency. For example, fewer elected representatives meant fewer seats to defend, fewer seats to defend meant less motivation for activists to knock on doors, less motivation meant a less active membership, and a less active membership meant an inability to seriously challenge incumbents, meaning fewer opportunities to return representatives. When you play out this picture across the post-coalition Scottish Liberal Democrats you can understand the problem more clearly. Not only had electoral representation shrunk but so had membership and resources. The geography of the party's membership was always patchy, with some areas having tiny numbers of members and activists. However, in recent years party membership went into decline. The party had 4,148 members at the end of 2010, but this had fallen to 3,080 in 2011 and then a low of 2,837 at the end of 2012.[1] This situation had effects on local campaigning as well as on the financial resources available to the party. Moreover, the electoral losses of 2011 had financial effects too. Before the Scottish election losses, the parliamentary party at Holyrood received £105,940.62 in public funds [Short money], after the 2011 election this amount fell to just £39,538 per annum. Party income of £511,406 in 2010 had fallen to £355,869 by the end of 2012, though the party remained in surplus. Its number of accounting units in Scotland had also fallen from 47 to 42 – meaning some local parties had financially declined beneath Electoral Commission registration levels. At the Scottish election in 2011, the Scottish Liberal Democrats spent £176,300 on the campaign when a much larger party. The Electoral Commission allocated the party a spending limit of £150,000 for the last 16 weeks of the referendum campaign [the regulated period]. Financing that as well as the various activities associated with the long campaign and the European Parliament election in the same year were a challenge for the party.

This situation was a problem for the party for a variety of reasons. First, because of the nature of electoral competition since devolution, parties faced an election almost every year – whether for UK, Scottish or European Parliaments or local authorities. This means that parties are constantly on election footing, and have to campaign almost all the time. Add in a referendum, and the issue is further complicated. For the large SNP membership, campaigning in an independence referendum was straightforward, despite its challenge and choices. The vast majority of the SNP membership subscribed to the party's *raison d'être*, and given the opportunity to deliver it, will gladly campaign for independence and sideline the opportunity to campaign for more partisan ends. The same cannot be said of Scottish Liberal Democrat activists, especially given the party's recent electoral record. While a federal UK was a long-standing party policy and the Liberal Democrats supported the Union, the party faced a dilemma of self-interest (meaning: survival) ahead of the referendum, with activists happy to deliver leaflets during the referendum campaign only inasmuch as they helped the party to retain seats in the future. The smaller size of the party membership compounded this problem. In short, the electoral decline of the Liberal Democrats had a negative impact upon their capacity to deliver activists on the ground to campaign in favour of the Union at the independence referendum, making the party more reliant upon the national campaign efforts of the UK government and Better Together.

Conclusion

The Scottish Liberal Democrats (and the Liberals before them) have long championed the cause of Home Rule for Scotland with devolution sitting comfortably with the twin principles of subsidiarity and federalism which guide so much of the party's constitutional policy. This support for Home Rule and, as it is currently conceptualised, fiscal federalism within the United Kingdom, made the Liberal Democrats' position in the constitutional debate around the referendum unique. For while they supported the Union – as their Labour and Conservative colleagues in the Better Together campaign did – they also supported a significant change to the wider UK constitution, something that their Unionist colleagues did not. The party articulated this position clearly and consistently through leader Willie Rennie's speeches to Liberal Democrat party conferences, carefully balancing positive remarks about the potential for Scotland to govern itself with the benefits of the Union and the perceived advantages that fiscal federalism would bring for both Scotland and the rest of the UK. Given that this was not an option that could be delivered at the 2014 independence referendum, this was undoubtedly a long-term strategy, which the Scottish Liberal Democrats hoped they would be able to deliver upon in the event of a 'No' vote in the referendum.

However, their ability to deliver Home Rule for Scotland was subject to several factors outwith the party's control. Firstly, there was a requirement for a 'No' vote in the referendum which was by no means guaranteed. Secondly, while the party was in a position of strength as junior coalition partners in the UK Government after 2010, the multi-level nature of politics in the UK created major electoral difficulties for the party at Scottish Parliamentary and local authority level, with a considerable reduction in both votes and seats at the respective elections in 2011 and 2012. Michael Moore's presence as Secretary of State for Scotland gave the party a prominent role in the debate over devolution reform and independence, and a role in influencing both the Scotland Act 2012 and the Edinburgh Agreement. However, this was no guarantee of electoral recovery for the party.

This chapter has examined the Scottish Liberal Democrats with regards to the campaign in the lead up to the independence referendum of 2014. The evolution of the party on the constitutional issue – major protagonists in the Scottish Constitutional Convention and the Yes-Yes campaign in the 1997 devolution referendum, junior coalition partners at Holyrood, the Steel, Calman and Campbell Commissions – has been considered in order to establish how the party have reached their current position on the constitutional question. The mixed fortunes the party has faced as a result of the multi-level nature of UK politics was also considered as a contributory factor in the Scottish Liberal Democrats' abilities to engage and influence the constitutional debate, while the three facets of their campaigning itself were also considered in their effectiveness.

Finally, the discourse utilised by the Scottish Liberal Democrats was analysed and the argument made that the party was attempting to build a third nodal point around which they hope that the constitutional debate will develop in the aftermath of the 2014 referendum. It is clear from the discourse that the Scottish Liberal Democrats occupy a unique position in the Scottish constitutional debate, wholeheartedly supporting neither option in the referendum but rather attempting to build support for a constitutional option – fiscal federalism – which was not currently on the political agenda. The party believed that by rejecting independence in the referendum, the opportunity would then arise at a later date to pursue this constitutional option, and that the referendum campaign allowed them to build the foundations of support for this principle by adopting a third nodal point – 'home rule' – in their referendum discourse to aid them in mapping out a Home Rule road to electoral recovery at future elections.

Bibliography

Bochel, John, David Denver and Allan Macartney [1982], *The Referendum Experience: Scotland 1979*, Aberdeen, Aberdeen University Press.
Bogdanor, Vernon [1998], *Devolution*, London, Opus.
Clark, Alistair [2012], *Political Parties in the UK*, Basingstoke, Palgrave Macmillan
Commission on Scottish Devolution [2009], *Serving Scotland Better: Scotland and the United Kingdom in the 21st Century – Final Report*, Edinburgh, Commission on Scottish Devolution.
Denver, David, James Mitchell, Charles Pattie and Hugh Bochel [1998], *Scotland* Decides, London, Frank Cass.
Devo Plus Group [2012], *A Stronger Scotland within the UK – First report of the Devo Plus Group*, Edinburgh, Devo Plus Group.
Harvey, Malcolm and Peter Lynch [2012], 'Getting to Yes: What Can Scottish Independence Campaigners Learn From the Devolution Referendums of 1979 and 1997?', Paper presented at the annual conference of the Political Studies Association, Belfast, 3-5 April, 2012.
Harvey, M. and Lynch, P. (2012), 'Inside the National Conversation: The SNP Government and the Politics of Independence 2007-2010', *Scottish Affairs* No. 80, Summer.
Harvie, Christopher and Peter Jones [2000], *The Road to Home Rule: Images of Scotland's Cause*, Edinburgh, Polygon.
HM Government [2012], *Scotland's Constitutional Future*, London, HMSO, Cmnd. 8203.
HM Government and Scottish Government [2012], *Agreement between the United Kingdom Government and the Scottish Government on*

a referendum on independence for Scotland, Edinburgh, Scottish Government.
Keating, Michael [2005], *The Government of Scotland: Public Policy Making after Devolution*, Edinburgh, Edinburgh University Press.
Laclau, Ernesto and Chantal Mouffe [1985], *Hegemony & Socialist Strategy*, London, Verso.
Lynch, Peter [1998], 'Third party politics in a four party system: the Liberal Democrats in Scotland' in *Scottish Affairs*, vol. 22, pp 16–32
Mitchell, James [2003], 'Third Year, Third First Minister' in Hazel, Robert (ed) [2003] *The State of the Nations 2003: The Third Year of Devolution in the United Kingdom*, Exeter, Imprint Academic.
Müller, Wolfgang C. and Kaare Strøm [1999], *Policy, Office or Votes? How Political Parties in Western Europe make hard decisions*, Cambridge, Cambridge University Press.
Rennie, Willie [2012a], *Speech to Scottish Liberal Democrat Conference*, 4 March 2012, online at: http://scotlibdems.org.uk/news/2012/03/sld-conference-willie-rennie-speech
Rennie, Willie [2012b], *Speech to Liberal Democrat Conference*, 25 September 2012, online at: http://scotlibdems.org.uk/news/2012/09/willie-rennie-speech-lib-dem-conference
Roddin, E [2004], 'Has the Labour Party or the Liberal Democrats Proved More Successful in the Partnership for Scotland Coalition? An Initial Assessment' in *Scottish Affairs*, vol. 48, pp 24–49.
Russell, Andrew and Edward Fieldhouse [2004], *Neither Left nor Right? The Liberal Democrats and the Electorate*, Manchester, Manchester University Press.
Scotland Office [2010], 'Moore publishes Bill to strengthen Scotland's future', 30 November, 2010, online at: https://www.gov.uk/government/news/moore-publishes-bill-to-strengthen-scotlands-future.
Scott, Tavish and Liam McArthur [2012], *Scotland's Constitutional Future – The Northern Isles*: a response to the UK Government's referendum consultation.
Scottish Labour Devolution Commission [2013], *Powers for a Purpose – Strengthening Devolution*, interim report, Glasgow, Scottish Labour Party
Scottish Labour Party and Scottish Liberal Democrats [2003], *A Partnership for a Better Scotland*, Edinburgh, Scottish Executive.
Scottish Liberal Democrats [2011], *Solutions for Scotland: Manifesto 2011*, Edinburgh, Scottish Liberal Democrats
Settle, Michael [2013], 'Scottish Lib Dem MPs fight to shake off taint of Tory links' in *The Herald*, Friday, 2 August, 2013, online

at: http://www.heraldscotland.com/politics/political-news/scottish-libdem-mps-fight-to-shake-off-taint-of-tory-links.21756154

The Home Rule and Community Commission of the Scottish Liberal Democrats [2012], *Federalism: The Best Future for Scotland*, Edinburgh, Scottish Liberal Democrats.

The Steel Commission [2006], *Moving to Federalism – A New Settlement for Scotland*, Edinburgh, Scottish Liberal Democrats.

Wallace, Jim [2008,], 'We must seize this opportunity to make devolution work', The Observer, 7 December, 2008.

Notes

1. Scottish Liberal Democrats, Statement of Accounts and Annual Report at 31st December 2012.

7

The Radical Parties and Independence: Another World is Possible?

Paul Gillen

Introduction

The SNP may be the senior partner in the Yes campaign but it was joined by the Scottish Green Party and the Scottish Socialist Party [SSP]. Both organisations became active participants in Yes and were also part of a broader mobilisation of the radical left in Scotland which saw the emergence of Labour for Independence, the Jimmy Reid Foundation, the Common Weal project and the Radical Independence movement formed in 2012. The road to supporting independence was as varied as the parties and organisations themselves, each treating the referendum campaign as a means to achieve a specific set of goals including independence as well as an awareness of what independence would mean for their political programmes. Significantly, these goals were based upon a plurality of alternative, more radical visions of independence as opposed to the moderate-left vision of the dominant SNP which included, at least initially, intentions to join NATO, keep the British Monarch as Head of State and retain the Pound Sterling as currency. Although the radical groups disagreed with the SNP over certain issues, each worked with the SNP and others within the Yes movement towards a Yes vote, attending meetings at the Yes Scotland headquarters in Glasgow, as well as canvassing and sharing platforms together across Scotland. This chapter will focus predominantly on the Greens and SSP, in relation to their autonomy position, referendum activities and discursive strategies, but also provide a brief analysis of the Radical Independence Campaign too, where some of the discourse of the radical left parties converged. The significance of these developments for the referendum and the political environment following the referendum was open to question given the relatively small size of the radical left parties in terms of membership, resources and political impact: though the symbolism of extending Yes into diverse groups and communities was clear.

The Evolution of Party Attitudes to the Autonomy Issue

The Scottish Green group was founded in the late 1970s by a group of activists in Edinburgh [as the Ecology Party in Scotland]. It remained a constituent part of the UK Green party until 1989, when it formally voted to form a separate Scottish party [Bennie, 2004:1]. Since 1990, the party has been campaigning for a 'clean environment, a healthy way of life and a peaceful world' [Scottish Green Party 1999]. For the Scottish Greens, this involved a commitment to 'a fairer, just society; for a safe environment; for peace not war; for healthy, strong communities.....for the public interest, not private profit above all else' [Baird and Harper, 2005]. The environment and action to tackle climate change were central to Scottish Green Party motivations (ibid). However, commitment to localism can be added as another key tenet of Green philosophy, for reasons that will be explored more fully below.

The Scottish Greens' formation was spurred by the electoral success of the party across the UK at the 1989 European election. From next to nothing electorally and organisationally, the party gained 14.5 per cent across the UK and 7.2 per cent in Scotland [Bennie 2002:102-3]. The party fielded candidates in all 8 Scottish European constituencies, winning 10.5 per cent in Edinburgh, 6.3 per cent in Glasgow and 9.5 per cent in the Highlands and islands. The result was a party with 1,250 members organised through 36 local parties [Bennie 2002:103]. And, the fact that the Scottish Greens were established as an independent party was to prove significant for the constitutional debate over the longer term, as the party moved to support independence and played its part in campaigning on the constitutional issue from 1992 onwards. Pre-devolution, Green electoral performance in Scotland was extremely limited due to the FPTP electoral system and the costs of elections.[1] However, that performance changed significantly in 1999 with the AMS electoral system that combined FPTP in constituencies but party list voting on regional lists using proportional representation. This change resulted in the Greens returning their first MSP in 1999, then leader Robin Harper (who made history by becoming the first elected Green to a Parliament in the UK). The Greens won 3.6 per cent in Scotland in 1999 [84,024 votes] but its 6.9 per cent in Edinburgh meant it gained one MSP. From then on, the Scottish Greens maintained a 'second vote' strategy, competing only on the regional lists and gaining continual representation at Holyrood at each election (Bennie, 2004:35). The election of Robin Harper was followed by even greater success in the 2003 Scottish Parliament Election, with 7 Green MSPs returned on 6.9 per cent of the vote [a peak of 132,138 votes]. However, the Greens declined in support at the 2007 Scottish Parliament Election to 4 per cent, losing five MSPs, though the party developed some post-election benefits by agreeing a policy cooperation agreement with the SNP minority government. In 2011 the Party again returned two MSPs on 4.4 per cent [87,060 votes, with a quarter of the total from Lothians alone] and the 2012 local elections also saw it elect 14 local councillors. These results also demonstrated the geographical strengths – and weaknesses – of the party, with 6 councillors in Edinburgh and 5 in Glasgow, to add to 1 MSP from each city.

One of the Greens' greatest successes to date came as a result of the party's support for the SNP after the 2007 Scottish Parliament elections. The Green MSPs agreed to support the appointment of Alex Salmond as First Minister, and in return, the SNP agreed to an early introduction of the Climate Change Bill and the appointment of co-convenor Patrick Harvie as chair of the Holyrood committee on Transport, infrastructure and climate change. However, despite some notable successes, Green Party membership remained comparatively small in number – just 1271 members at the end of 2012.[2] Indeed, small Party membership and relatively few votes in elections has been a running theme for the Scottish Greens, as demonstrated by Lynn Bennie's study on Green Party membership (2004:204). In 1979, the Party had just 100 members. This rose to 1250 in 1990, but in 1993, there was a drastic decline to just 200 members. The rise in party membership since then was attributed to increased coverage of environmental issues by the media, and improvements in the party's weak internal organisation. Electoral success and the strong profile gained by MSPs like Robin Harper – the first elected Green politician in the UK – were seen to boost party membership and organisation (Kuin, 2006:139), with those joining the Greens seen to be economically 'well off' (2004:205).

Although the Scottish Greens voted to officially support independence in October 2013, this was only by a two-to-one majority at the vote at party conference. Part of the reason for this was due to competing interpretations of the meaning of independence. For example, Green language around the autonomy issue had changed and varied with some members championing autonomy over independence whilst others spoke of independence from a decentralisation point of view and from a position that believed independence to be a means of delivering a more sustainable economy.[3] This internal reality explained the less than rigid Green discursive strategy during the referendum campaign, and indicated that the party may not have been as fully behind independence as the Radical Independence Campaign, the SSP or the SNP: though its party conference in 2012 did support a radical version of independence and participation in Yes Scotland.

Significantly, the Scottish Greens officially believed that 'Scotland should be an independent state, not as an end in itself......but in order to have the levers available to achieve "a greener and fairer society, working in partnership with our sister nations in the UK, Europe and across the World."' (Scottish Green Party 2012). The idea that independence was a means to an end was likely to be influenced by the Greens' belief in the need to de-centralise government (Scottish Green Party 1999), its opposition to Trident in Scotland and to membership of pro-Trident NATO, as well as support of 'fairer taxation' in the form of a land value tax (LVT), a revitalised NHS which would have a 'new focus on prevention of ill-health' and to set an example with regards to fair trade, debt-relief, tackling climate change and challenging 'military-led foreign policy.' (ibid). Imagining this type of transformation under Westminster rule was seen to be impossible due to UK 'posturing' on the global stage with regards to military intervention amongst other issues. By contrast, independence was seen to represent a 'far better' chance to decentralise power, and a better prospect for examining the role of the public sector with regards to infrastructure and ownership of industry and public transport.[4]

The Scottish Socialist Party (SSP) was founded in 1998, and defines itself as being '...built on solidarity and the spirit of resistance to oppression, injustice and nasty con tricks that strangle communities and people's lives.' (Scottish Socialist Party, 2011:5). The Party has two co-spokespersons – Colin Fox and Sandra Webster – and contested the first elections to the newly established Scottish Parliament in 1999, when it gained its first MSP, then National Convenor Tommy Sheridan. In the 2003 Scottish Parliament elections, the Party gained an additional five regional list MSPs: Frances Curran, Rosie Kane, Carolyn Leckie, Colin Fox, and Rosemary Byrne. This success came off the back of the SSP's anti-Iraq War campaign and indicated an appetite from the Scottish electorate for a principled Scottish Socialist Party (Gonzalez, 2006). However, when it came to the 2007 Scottish Parliament Election, the SSP had undergone a political crisis and split (fuelled by the Tommy Sheridan controversy), leaving the Party with no MSPs.[5] The SSP did not return any MSPs in the 2011 Scottish

Parliament election either, when the party stood on every regional list (Scottish Socialist Party 2011:5). Party membership shrank from 3000 at its peak in 2007 (Kane, 2007:57) and the SSP had approximately 600 members in August 2013,[6] partly due to the aftermath of the Sheridan affair and the emergence of Solidarity as a radical left competitor for the SSP. At the 2011 Scottish election the SSP had faced electoral competition from Solidarity in 7 of the 8 regional lists [except Glasgow, where Solidarity let George Galloway and Respect lead the list, to no avail] as well as the Socialist Labour Party. However, the radical left parties fared badly at the 2011 election. The SSP won only 0.42 per cent, the Socialist Labour Party won 0.85 per cent and Solidarity won only 0.14 percent. So in electoral terms, the far left had fallen very far from 2003 and the SSP were only able to muster 8,272 votes in the Scottish election.[7]

The genesis of the SSP was fairly simple. It was formed through a series of mergers and alliances but had its origins in the Militant Tendency within the Labour Party in the 1980s. After a series of expulsions from Labour, the faction created Scottish Militant Labour and, allied with the Anti-Poll Tax federation, started to create a dedicated political organisation that saw some electoral prominence in 1992 – when Tommy Sheridan became a Glasgow councillor when resident in an Edinburgh prison for non-payment of a fine [Bennie 2002:100]. From then on, SML morphed into the Scottish Socialist Alliance and then the SSP. These changes involved huge changes in strategy, 'separation' from UK political organisations and the broadening of the far left on issues and personnel. It also saw the new SSP emerge to benefit from devolution and electoral system change and become a pro-independence party. This latter development was facilitated by the fact that the SSA favoured devolution and ultimately independence, but Arthur Scargill and his Socialist Labour Party (SLP) were 'lukewarm' over the idea of independence – hence ruling out a left merger. Therefore, it was decided that a new party (the SSP) should be set up in order to work progressively for Scottish independence and the removal of 'British Imperialism' in Scotland.[8] From the outset, the party was committed to 'an independent socialist Scotland, a modern democratic republic' [Scottish Socialist Party 2013:7].

The new party was committed to an 'Independent Socialist Scotland', believing that certain Party/Socialist goals could be fulfilled if independence was achieved through a Yes vote. These goals broadly included: 'A directly elected Constitutional Assembly, representative of Scotland's regional, gender and ethnic diversity...which would be put to a further referendum vote', a nuclear-free Scotland which would stay out of NATO, a reduction in military spending of £2.5 billion, a new relationship with the European Union, the abolition of the monarchy, no unelected second chamber, all elections to be conducted under proportional representation, full citizenship for all living in Scotland, and 'A socialist Scotland, based on the principles of equality, democracy, liberty, generosity and solidarity' (Scottish Socialist Party, 2011:10). However, one of the underpinning elements of the SSP's referendum campaign strategy was to oppose the 'Bedroom Tax' and this became a popular trend for the SSP during the campaign.

Although the SSP did support independence, as indicated by the tensions between the SSA and SLP, the Scottish left's relationship with independence was not straightforward: far from it. For example, the left in Scotland was caught in two minds over independence. On one hand, Labour and the Communist Party of Britain (CPB) believed that independence 'would disunite the British working class and only go to serve the interests of the bourgeoisie' (Cornock, 2013:1). The left was clearly divided on the constitutional issue with some expression of support for the UK state as 'political mobilisation has to be conceived and constructed at the British level' [Foster and Leonard 2013:11]. On the other hand, the SSP and Communist Party of Scotland (CPS) believed that in order for progressive socialism to flourish in Scotland (and in England), a break with the British state was a precondition (Cornock 2013:1, Communist Party of Scotland 2013). However, according to Colin Fox, the SSP had always been comfortable in supporting independence,[9] which made it relatively easy for the party to join Yes Scotland, with Colin Fox serving on the organisation's advisory board.

Party Strategy for the Referendum and its Aftermath

Participation in Yes Scotland offered challenges for both the Greens and the SSP. In terms of membership, organisation, resources and presence, the minor parties were eclipsed by the SNP. The substantial initial role played by the SNP in Yes Scotland's establishment and early operation made the organisation less of a multi-party body: due to staff transfers, financing and strategy. However, in time, Yes Scotland became more genuinely multi-party, with Green and SSP involvement at different levels and active involvement in the advisory board. Yes Scotland was seen to involve a complex balance in order to function properly with a default position of looking to the Scottish Government for advice on specific issues: part of the organisational triangle of Yes. Coordination between the different levels and the different components of the Yes campaign was therefore a challenge but improved over time. For both the Greens and SSP, involvement in a broad, well-organised Yes campaign exposed them to new styles of campaigning and organisation but also provided them with opportunities to appear in front of new political audiences through public meetings and TV debates, widening the reach of each party within traditional and new communities and allowing them a new prominence and platform in spite of their modest size.

For the SSP, participation in Yes Scotland was very direct. The SSP was in Yes Scotland for a part in a referendum victory that the party had worked for over the last 15-16 years. The referendum campaign would allow the party to raise its political profile, connect its ideology to independence and change and be part of a coalition opposed to welfare cuts and austerity. However, defeat at the referendum would be a big blow to the party too, as the party's involvement in the campaign meant it was playing for big political stakes. Yes Scotland was an important organisation for the SSP in a bid to secure independence and further support. And the links with Yes Scotland and the referendum brought encouragement to the party during the long referendum campaign as it made the party feel that its prospects were 'rosy' and that its best days were ahead of it.

Thus, the relationship with Yes Scotland was important for the SSP and the SSP's role within Yes Scotland gave the party a new lease of life. The referendum campaign was the SSP's chance to step out of the shadows and grow, even though a lot of people had written the party off following the Sheridan controversy in 2006. The party was aware that the SNP were the biggest suppliers of finance and Yes canvassers but sought to play their part on the ground. However, it was clear that the SSP wished that it could become more involved in the referendum campaign by supplying more canvassers and money, but the party's size made financial contributions difficult: it had total income of just £36,032 in 2012 for example and a small membership base. Despite this, the party was represented on the Yes Scotland advisory board, which met around every two months initially. More broadly, SSP representatives took the discussion on independence to other members of the SSP as well as speaking at public events raising concerns and other matters with party members, supporters and members of the public.

Partisan Motives, Goals and Behaviours During the Long Referendum Campaign

Campaigning on behalf of a Yes vote was challenging for the Greens and SSP given the small size of the parties. As a result of membership distribution, the Greens were more active in some geographical areas than in others: particularly in areas such as Edinburgh and Glasgow West and the party had only 15 organised local groups in total at the time of writing. The party was also aware of two things. First, that its own membership needed to be mobilised over independence in order to increase support and activity levels on the ground. Second, that there were Green voters who needed to be 'courted' on the independence issues to that they would understand how Green politics would best be served with a Yes vote. Whilst some local branches had produced and distributed leaflets on forthcoming events in local areas (for example, the Greenlight events organised by the Edinburgh Greens branch), the Greens' own referendum output could never be on the same scale as the SNP's. For example, the party had limited financial resources and did not have a specific referendum fund at the time of writing, although a fundraising plan was under development.[10] Though the Electoral Commission rules allowed the party to spend a maximum of £150,000 in the regulated period for the last 16 weeks of the referendum campaign, it was hard to see the party spending anything like that.

Despite being part Yes Scotland, the Greens intended to set up their own pro-independence campaign, with a launch date around November 2013 [Green Yes was launched on 15th November 2013 and it experienced a small boom in party membership applications after this]. The rationale for a Green independence campaign was simple: it was believed that a transformation in society was needed rather than management of the same centre-right model, and this led to the belief within the party that a campaign with a slightly different style and tone from Yes Scotland and the SNP was required: more in line with the radical independence perspective outlined below in this chapter. The Greens were critical of the SNP's focus on a commitment to keep the British Monarch as Head of State in an independent Scotland and over its commitment to NATO membership after independence.[11] Finally, the Greens felt that whether there was a Yes or No vote in September 2014, the SNP would need to redefine itself as a political party and that would provide a political opportunity for the Greens, with the creation of a new political space comprised of centre-left and environmentally-concerned SNP supporters.

In relation to campaigning on the independence referendum, much of the SSP's work took place at public events. Some of these were the traditional SSP public meetings – with attendance boosted by the combined impact of the referendum and bedroom tax. However, the party also received numerous invitations to speak at Yes events across Scotland as the local Yes groups were established across the country in recognition of its role in Yes Scotland and links to the trade unions.

Colin Fox and/or Sandra Webster were frequent speakers at these events, outlining the Scottish Socialist case for Independence. Themes included the 'Bedroom Tax', unemployment and the UK coalition government as well as independence. Public meetings took place in Dundee, Edinburgh and Glasgow, amongst other areas and the SSP even had a fringe meeting at the October 2012 SNP Conference in Perth. Public meetings were a key element to the SSP's grassroots activity, and this was no different when it came to supporting independence.

In terms of party referendum finance, the aim was to get total funds as close as possible to £50,000 but the party acknowledged that this was a 'huge ask'. The SSP's approach to party finance was to spend it as they get it. The party did have a referendum fund which began in Autumn 2012 and would be utilised. Fox pointed to the SSP's election funding process as an indicator of how the SSP built and spent funds. The party received mostly small donations but had received bigger donations from sympathisers in the arts, for example. One of the most profound aspects of the SSP's relationship with Yes was that the party had been warmly welcomed as part of Yes Scotland. Fox recalled that he had 'never once heard anybody say the SSP isn't taking its share'. The hard work of the SSP as well as an attitude of if we lose, 'we couldn't have given any more' was part of that.[12] There was a strong impression of mutual respect between the SSP and those within Yes Scotland, at least from the SSP's perspective.

The Discursive Strategies Adopted by Party Actors

Unlike the SNP which had a 'nodal point' (see Howarth and Stavrakakis, 2000:8) of 'independence', the Scottish Greens had a stringently ideological 'nodal point' of 'Green' (see Stavrakakis, 2000:101). Alongside this nodal point, the Greens articulated a chain of equivalence using empty signifiers (see Howarth and Stavrakakis, 2000:9), in order to dominate both the meaning of these signifiers, and to articulate a specific vision of independence. Take the following quote from Patrick Harvie, for example:

> Most Greens agree there will be far more opportunities to advance our core values of sustainability, fairness and peace with a Yes vote in the referendum. The well-worn Green maxim that 'small is beautiful' applies to many of the positive arguments for independence. (Harvie, 27th August 2013b).

Here, Harvie articulated 'independence' in a chain of equivalence alongside the empty signifiers 'sustainability', 'fairness', 'peace' and decentralisation (as indicated by the phrase 'small is beautiful'), thus articulating 'independence' as a logical goal of the Greens, and those signifiers as key components of support for independence. As will be shown throughout this section, this Green vision of independence was articulated as an alternative to the SNP's dominant vision of independence, and of course to Westminster rule in order to prepare the party for the outcome of the referendum, whether Yes or No. This will be shown by breaking Green discourse down into three key issue-areas: (1) localism, (2) the economy and welfare, (3) environment, which covered the values of sustainability, fairness, peace and decentralisation.

Localism

The Greens believed that Scotland should be able to control 'more of its own destiny' (Scottish Green Party 2012), and this through the medium of independence was a central element of Green referendum strategy. A commitment to government on a local scale had been a long standing commitment of the Scottish Greens, believing that localism made politics and the economy work better – 'The Greens believe that our economies and our politics work best on a more local scale.' (Scottish Green Party, 2011:6). Thus, the Scottish Greens not only believed in power being 'handed down' from UK-level to Holyrood, but from Holyrood to local councils, then onto communities (Scottish Green Party, 2012). In a piece by Patrick Harvie on the Yes Scotland online blog, he further elucidated this stance:

> Greens have a longstanding commitment to decentralisation. For democracy to be strong it's important that people feel a sense of connection with the decisions that affect them, and that's best achieved with active participation in local decisions. Unlike many of the small independent northern European countries that Scotland is often compared to, we have a very low level of participation in decision-making and a very centralised form of government. That could have changed with devolution, but instead we've seen ever more power sucked up from local level and brought to St Andrew's House. So we Greens see independence not simply as withdrawal from the UK – it's about recognising that political power starts at local level and should only be passed up the chain where there's a powerful reason to do so (Harvie, 10th January 2013).

The above passage captures perfectly Green thinking on localism and the referendum. Patrick Harvie attempted to create a political frontier (see Howarth and Stavrakakis, 2000:9) between the Scottish Greens and the UK, and simultaneously between the Scottish Greens and the SNP-Scottish government. First, Harvie set out the positive, Green case for devolving more power to local level. He constructed a positive chain of equivalence using signifiers including 'Greens', 'independence' 'longstanding', 'decentralisation', 'democracy', 'strong', 'important', 'people', 'connection', 'decisions', 'best', 'active participation', 'local', with the overall effect of articulating 'independence' as a form of 'decentralisation', which was a 'strong' path, that the Greens have always stood for, and it would lead to enhanced 'democracy' in Scotland because 'local' 'people' would be able to have 'active participation' in decision-making.

Harvie contrasted that vision with an articulation of the system of government in Scotland both as part of the UK and under a devolved SNP administration. He built a negative chain of equivalence, weaving the 'UK' into an articulation of the system as inadequate because of a 'very low level of participation in decision-making and a very centralised form of government', the signifiers 'low' and 'centralised' being essential in the negative articulation of the system of government. Additionally, Harvie articulated the Scottish government (presumably this includes both Labour and SNP administrations), as being a cause of further centralisation even though devolution could have brought decentralisation (according to Harvie) – 'That could have changed with devolution, but instead we've seen ever more power sucked up from local level and brought to St Andrew's House.'. Here, 'centralised' is treated as an empty signifier – Harvie conferred a negative meaning onto it, and articulated is as a negative feature of the UK government. Thus, the political frontier articulated by Patrick Harvie consisted of a negative chain of equivalence, attaching centralisation of power to consecutive UK and Scottish governments, and contrasting this with a positive chain of equivalence, articulating 'decentralisation' via 'independence' as the democratic alternative for a small nation such as Scotland. By doing so, Patrick Harvie articulated 'decentralisation' as a key component of the Green's vision of an independent Scotland.

The Economy and Welfare

The Scottish Greens articulated economic and welfare policy together closely and that both were untenable at UK level. The alternative was articulated as a transformation in the economy based on the principles of the empty signifier 'Green economy': 'health', 'relationships', 'equality' and 'community', which could be best achieved through 'independence'. The party constructed a negative chain of equivalence, which included the UK government and parties, as well as the SNP-Scottish government, in order to articulate them as being detrimental to the economy and to welfare including public services and equality. Take the following passage for example:

> The recent recession has been a tough time for many people, but astonishingly the other political parties seem determined to re-float the same failed economic model. To do so, they will cut public spending rather than raise taxes on those who can afford to pay...Labour and Tory governments alike have fostered this inequality, on the assumption that economic growth benefits everyone eventually. This great lie of the unfettered free market cannot be allowed to stand (Scottish Green Party, 2010:5).

By articulating the economic recession in Britain in the same negative chain of equivalence as the 'Labour and Tory governments' and their resolve to 're-float the same failed economic model' which included cutting 'public spending', the Greens attempted to articulate successive UK governments as allowing the gap between rich and poor to grow, fostering 'inequality'. Added to the negative chain of equivalence on economy and welfare was the SNP-Scottish government:

> The Greens believe the SNP Budget that was passed, with Coalition support, failed to protect Scotland from the Tory cuts, and that an alternative is urgently needed (Scottish Green Party, 2011:4).

Although the Scottish government had a low level of manoeuvrability in economic and welfare policy, something that the Scottish Greens acknowledged (Scottish Green Party, 2011:4), the Scottish Greens did have one eye on the 2016 Holyrood election in particular, so inevitably attempted to distinguish themselves from the nationalist SNP by linking the 'SNP budget' in a negative chain of equivalence with the 'coalition' and 'Tory cuts' (Scottish Green Party, 2011:4) in order to naturalise the idea that the SNP, like the UK government, could not be trusted with economic and welfare policy, leaving the Greens as a viable alternative.

On the other side of the political frontier came this alternative, based on 'Green economics':

> Green economics offer a radical and positive alternative, grounded in a desire to put human wellbeing and a safe environment at the

top of government priorities. We believe that economic policy must place value not just on material wealth, but on the things which truly make life worth living – our health, our relationships, our human need to co-operate and create a sense of equality and community. (Scottish Green Party, 2010:4).

'Green economics' is treated here as an empty signifier, and by articulating 'Green economics' alongside signifiers including 'radical', 'positive', 'human wellbeing', 'safe environment', 'health', 'relationships', 'equality' and 'community' in a positive chain of equivalence, the Greens attempted to create a relatable subject position, based on a wide array of values including equality, environmentalism and localism. And if there was any doubt that this strategy did not necessarily fit into the Scottish Green's referendum strategy, Patrick Harvie as a Green co-convenor clarifies:

I'll be voting Yes out of a conviction that the transformation needed in our society and our economy – a transformation that I believe Green politics represents – can best be achieved by Scotland as a small independent country (Patrick Harvie, 10th January 2013).

Thus, 'independence' was articulated as the best vehicle to achieve a transformation in economic and welfare policy affecting Scotland, an economic policy which was articulated as a 'political failure' at UK-level because it fostered 'poverty' and the 'frenzied and destructive behaviour of the City' (Scottish Green Party 2010:3), as well as a welfare system that was being dismantled (Scottish Green Party, 2010:4). However, the Greens also articulated the SNP-Scottish government as part of the same negative chain of equivalence, indicating a belief that social and economic change was needed at both UK level through independence, but at Scottish government level by having further Green representation at Holyrood.

The Environment

Finally, as may be expected, the environment was an important aspect of Green referendum policy (as it is with Green policy around Europe), and there was a commitment to ensuring that the environment was at the centre of politics and 'not an afterthought' (Scottish Green Party, 2010:6). In particular, the Scottish Greens articulated climate change as '...the most urgent threat to the survival of humanity', with the poorest in society both at home and internationally facing the brunt of the threat (Scottish Green Party, 2010:6). Action to tackle climate change (and thus a 'greener world') was articulated as an opportunity to fulfil a guarantee of 'human wellbeing and social justice around the world', with transformation being experienced in 'many areas of life' including energy, transport, food, homes and buildings, as well as in communities and the shaping of them. This paved the way to tackle environmental injustice and to bring about 'a more equal society and achieve a better quality of life for everyone.' (Scottish Green Party, 2010:6).

In relation to the referendum, the Scottish Greens attacked the UK government by constructing a negative chain of equivalence between the UK government and action to tackle climate change:

> The Copenhagen conference on climate change was a disgraceful letdown, with Governments from around the world refusing to take the steps which are needed. Even more disturbingly, the UK joined with a handful of other governments to present their 'Copenhagen Accord', which contained no commitment to binding cuts, no solutions for developing countries, and no prospect of safeguarding the world against the crucial 2-degree warming threshold (Scottish Green Party, 2010:6).

By utilising signifiers and phrases including 'Copenhagen conference', 'climate change', 'disgraceful let down', 'refusing', 'disturbingly', 'UK', 'no commitment to binding cuts', 'no solutions' and 'no prospect', it is clear that the Scottish Greens attempted to tie the UK government to what was articulated as inaction on climate change at international level. And this fitted into the Scottish Green's overall referendum strategy by articulating the UK government as unwilling to take the steps needed to tackle climate change, with the solution to this being independence. The Scottish Greens added the Scottish government to the negative chain of equivalence on inaction on climate change:

> On many issues, Greens part company with others in the pro-independence movement. We'll never be a party that wants to position itself as a friend to the oil industry for example. But pro-fossil-fuel policy has been coming from government after government at UK level, not just from recent Scottish governments – tax breaks for oil companies, permissions for opencast expansion and political support for the development of new "unconventional" fossil fuel sources, such as deepwater

oil drilling, coal bed methane and fracking for shale gas (Patrick Harvie, 10th February 2013).

Thus, both the UK and the Scottish government were articulated negatively with actions that the Scottish Greens articulated as harming the environment, including 'tax breaks for oil companies', 'deepwater oil drilling', and 'fracking'. Additionally, Patrick Harvie articulated the actions of the UK government as contrary to a peaceful World:

> Instead of blowing billions on the military we could look afresh at defence and ask ourselves ... in a world where the real threats to human security have more to do with food, water, energy and climate than they have to do with borders, who needs to be defended and from what? (Harvie, 10th February 2013).

Harvie constructed a political frontier by stating that the Greens 'part company' with such actions and offering an alternative 'Green approach':

> The Green approach will move us away from fossil fuels and towards local supply of energy. Local community heating schemes, combined heat and power and micro-generation have the potential to secure energy supply while reducing carbon emissions, but only if we also invest in a "smart grid" and support large scale renewables too (Scottish Green Party, 2010:6).

'Green approach' is understood here as an empty signifier, and by articulating 'Green economics' in a positive chain of equivalence with signifiers including 'secure energy supply', 'reducing carbon emissions', and support of 'large scale renewables', the Greens attempted to create a subject position that environmentally aware/concerned people could relate to and thus choose the Greens and 'independence' as an alternative to the inaction on environmental issues by the UK parties/government and the SNP-Scottish government.

After examination, it is clear that the nature of SSP referendum discourse was based upon the articulation of an Independent Socialist Scotland built upon the 'social democratic values held by the majority of people who live here (Scotland)' (Fox, 3rd June 2013). Indeed, it was a common SSP articulatory practise to attempt to naturalise the idea that the majority of Scotland's residents held social democratic values in order to present the SSP as the party to represent those values. Therefore, 'socialism' acted as the ideological nodal point that occupied the structural position of SSP discourse.

The referendum campaign was intriguing for the SSP because it was seen as a means to revive the SSP both in terms of membership, and electoral success after the referendum. The SSP attempted to construct a political frontier between UK and Scottish political parties and governments on one hand and the SSP on the other. This strategy continued before and through-out the long referendum campaign. Consider the following two passages, for example:

> Instead, New Labour, the SNP and the Tory/LibDem [sic] coalition made the choice to cut public services, cut pensions and cut benefit levels to pay for the crisis. The Scottish Socialist Party has a different approach. We are on your side, not the side of the rich and powerful (Scottish Socialist Party, 2011:6).

By articulating past and present UK and Scottish governments as well as the parties that ran those administrations in a negative chain of equivalence with 'the rich and powerful', public service cuts, pension cuts and benefit cuts, the SSP created an 'other', in order to allow the SSP to articulate itself as the party that was 'different', the party that was 'on your [the working class's] side' thus creating a subject position with which people who were working class/less well-off could relate. There are several examples of this throughout the SSP's 2011 Holyrood Manifesto, and though-out SSP discourse. Take the following passage, for example:

> Whilst the Yes campaign has sought to highlight the possibilities to advance Scotland's social democratic values and aspirations the No side has offered a diet of unremitting negativity and doom-mongering. Be that as it may. The left's case for Independence is that the opportunity to break with the British state, its Westminster Parliament, its Whitehall mandarins, its City of London capitalists, its Bank of England financiers and its South East England political exclusivity would undoubtedly benefit the Scottish working class. Socialists here make a clear case for Scottish Independence based on extending the unmistakeable social democratic values held by the majority of people who live here. These values are constantly subverted by a political, economic and social elite we can neither influence nor change. (Fox, 3rd June 2013).

The 'British State' is understood here as an empty signifier, and it was articulated in a negative chain of equivalence with 'capitalists', 'financiers' and 'political exclusivity' on one side of a political frontier in order to subvert the economic and political climate in 'Westminster' and the 'City of London'. On the other side of the political frontier, 'independence' was articulated as a means to achieve the SSP's goal of advancing 'Scotland's social democratic values and aspirations' and helping the 'Scottish working class'. The similarities and differences between the first and second passage are clear. In the second passage, the same negative chain of equivalence was articulated between the 'British State' and the SSP which was standing up for the 'Scottish working class'. The extra variable – and one clear difference - in the second passage is the signifier 'independence', and that by working for independence, the SSP was standing up for the 'social democratic values' of the 'majority of people' who lived in Scotland. Significantly, Fox arguably extended his articulation of a working class subject position to include both the 'Scottish working class' and anyone living in Scotland who felt that they held 'social democratic values'. As such, 'Scottish working class' is an empty signifier that the SSP attempted to dominate the meaning of in order to secure the support of those who saw themselves as a member of the 'Scottish working class', or who were sympathetic.

Therefore, the SSP's discursive strategy for the referendum consisted of an articulation of a political frontier designed to frame the independence debate as one between City of London capitalism and South East of England political exclusivity and the 'Scottish working class' that the SSP stood up for. On one side, a negative chain of equivalence was articulated between the 'rich and powerful', cuts to public services, pensions and benefits made by the UK and Scottish governments, the SNP, the Unionist parties (Labour, Conservatives, Liberal Democrats), Capitalists in the 'City of London', 'Bank of England financiers', 'unremitting negativity' from the No campaign and a politically exclusive atmosphere in the South East of England. On the other side, a positive chain of equivalence was articulated between 'socialism' 'independence', the SSP, the 'Scottish working class', 'advancing Scotland's social democratic values', 'better things', and a 'different approach'. This was an attempt not only to naturalise 'socialism' as the way forward for Scotland, but to naturalise independence as the means to achieve the Scotland that the 'Scottish working class' aspired to – in fact, independence was articulated as the only way to realising a Socialist Scotland and removing British Imperialism, thus attempting to provide closure to an incomplete system.

The Radical Independence Campaign

The Radical Independence Campaign (RIC) was a grassroots organisation, which promoted independence as a means to a 'better Scotland', and for many of its members, a Scotland based on leftist principles. For RIC, this translated into 'a Nordic-style universal welfare state with mixed economy model' and 'policies designed to spread national wealth as evenly as possible' (Scottish Left Review, 2012). It was a coalition of '...socialists, feminists, trade unionists, Greens, peace movement, poverty campaigners, anti-racist groups, community activists, civil liberty campaigners and more who believed independence offered Scotland its best hope of a progressive future' (Scottish Left Review, 2012), and in time it constituted part of the Yes Scotland campaign.

RIC began as the Radical Independence *Conference* at Glasgow's Radisson Blu Hotel on 24th November 2012. The conference was attended by almost 900 people and involved plenary and workshop sessions. It featured an array of political and civic society figures including Conference organisers Robin McAlpine (director of the Jimmy Reid Foundation and editor of the Scottish Left Review) and Jonathon Shafi (a co-founder of Radical Independence), Independent MSP Jean Urquhart, Scottish Green Party co-convenor and MSP Patrick Harvie, Chairman of Yes Scotland Dennis Canavan, and writer and commentator Gerry Hassan. One of the highlights from the Conference was a Radical Independence Declaration, which was drafted by Robin McAlpine and delivered by musician and Yes Scotland Advisory Board member, Pat Kane. The Declaration stipulated that Radical Independence 'is not a campaign for independence', rather for a 'better Scotland', which it is believed could begin only with independence as a starting point (Radical Independence Campaign, 2012).

The Declaration also set out the Radical Independence vision of a 'better Scotland', which included Scotland as a participative democracy, where the many rather than the few took decisions, as a society of equals, where poverty was not accepted, as having a 'just economy', where profit did not justify damaging people or the environment, with a 'great welfare state' that consisted of a social contact between the people rather than between the people and the state, as a 'good neighbour' in helping resolve global inequality, climate change and conflict, and finally as a moral nation, where emphasis was placed on 'mutuality, cooperation and fellowship' (Radical Independence Campaign 2012).

Since the Conference in November 2012, the Radical Independence Campaign sought to develop an organisation and events around Scotland. It launched peoples' assemblies, organised a tour of the country and established 18 different local campaign groups. The UK government's welfare reforms were a particular focus of its campaigning, with RIC involvement in the protests against the 'bedroom tax' in Glasgow and Edinburgh on 30th March 2013 and organising the 'Stop the bedroom tax' in Easterhouse meetings in April 2012. On the 25th April 2013, the Campaign held a 'People's Independence Assembly' in Edinburgh, with speakers including Trade Unionist Cat Boyd, Scottish disability rights campaigner Susan Archibald, Bella Caledonia contributor Kevin Williamson, and Green MSP Alison Johnstone. Each set out their own reasons for taking part in the campaign, as well as their visions for Scotland post-independence. And on 23rd November 2013, RIC held its second RIC Conference in Glasgow.

RIC believed that it was time for the Scottish Left to start offering hope, rather than to hope for change. It believed that those living in Scotland were experiencing the No campaign's vision of the future i.e. the status quo. The campaign emerged because of a perceived failure of the British State, and of the Labour Party's inability to change how the British State functioned. And the independence referendum gave those on the Scottish Left renewed enthusiasm and optimism that a 'better Scotland' could be achieved without impediment by the British State − 'The British State is and always will be a machine for transferring power and wealth from the many to the few' (Scottish Left Review, 2012).

RIC discourse attempted to construct a political frontier between the British establishment and the Scottish Left. It attempted to subvert 'London' rule which was articulated as exclusive, greedy and corrupt, but also attempted to articulate a specific vision of Scotland's future − One that offered a style of independence that was different to the vision offered by the SNP. By doing so, RIC attempted to create a subject position that those of the Scottish Left could relate to. This indicates that the RIC's discursive strategy was to convince the Scottish Left, through framing, that independence would be the best means to achieve not only socialism in Scotland, but a fresh start, and that there was an alternative to the vision of independence that was offered by the SNP. Additionally, it is argued here that RIC also had a nodal point of 'socialism', but this version of socialism was slightly different to that of the SSP's by placing more of an emphasis on a 'Nordic-style' welfare state, and a 'mixed-economy'.

On one side of the political frontier, RIC constructed a negative chain of equivalence, articulating 'London' as a place of wealth, greed, exclusivity and military aggression:

> London is one of the world centres of wrongness. It is one of the great centres of destructive finance acting not only as a home for corruption but politically as one of its great global enforcers. It is one of the centres of arms dealing. It is the command and control centre for one of the world's more aggressive militaries with its weapons of indiscriminate civilian extermination. It is the

beachhead for attacks on the European social model by (mainly US) corporations. It is a city-state dominated by new money and old, a club of private school boys who have built a haven for wealthy Russian criminals (Scottish Left Review, 2012).

Signifiers including 'wrongness', 'destructive finance', 'corruption', 'arms dealing', 'aggressive militaries', 'civilian extermination' and 'private school' were articulated together in this negative chain of equivalence along with the empty signifier 'London' in order to dominate the meaning of 'London' rule both economically and politically. By doing so, RIC articulated the economics and politics of 'London' as negative and against the values of Scotland. The SNP was added to the negative chain of equivalence: 'Few of us are happy about the drift of the SNP's badly-sown-together patchwork of a vision...' (Scottish Left Review, 2012). Thus, RIC articulated 'London' rule and the SNP's vision of independence as contrary to the vision of RIC.

On the other side of the political frontier, RIC articulated its vision of independence in a positive chain of equivalence:

This vision says 'let's look for the best bits of the best societies we can find and move Scotland quickly in that direction. From there we can see further still'. What we want is a Nordic-style universal welfare state with mixed economy model. We want policies designed to spread national wealth as evenly as possible. We want an open, transparent society which puts human rights and civil liberties to the fore. And we want a benign and collegiate foreign policy which seeks to put Scotland in a global lead position on disarmament, conflict resolution, reducing climate change, tackling global inequality and making global trade and global institutions fairer (Scottish Left Review, 2012).

Signifiers including 'Nordic-style', 'universal welfare state', 'mixed economy', 'evenly as possible', 'open', 'transparent', 'disarmament, 'conflict resolution', 'reducing climate change', 'tackling global inequality' and 'fairer' were utilised in order to confer meaning onto 'independence' – that independence could lead to a society based on leftist values rather than the SNP's 'patchwork of a vision' which included Scottish membership of NATO, keeping the British Pound as Scotland's currency and the British Monarch as Scotland's Head of State. Thus, RIC framed the SNP vision of independence as inadequate or not going far enough, and 'London' rule as exclusive, corrupt and aggressive in order to contrast with the RIC's articulation of a more radical independence as leading to a 'fairer', more 'open' and 'transparent' Scotland. RIC articulated a subject position that attempted to appeal to those who agreed that the Union and the SNP's vision of independence did not work in the best interests of those (socialists/ members of the Scottish working class) living in Scotland, framing RIC's radical vision of independence as a viable alternative.

Conclusion

Each party and organisation covered in this chapter offered alternative visions of independence from each other and from the SNP, although there was a clear crossover as these visions were left-leaning. Each was careful to maintain the stance that they were not SNP fronts, and that their visions of independence were different to the SNP's. This is not only because of ideological differences within the broad Yes coalition, but because each was attempting to strengthen its position before 2015 Westminster elections and 2016 Scottish Parliament elections. The Scottish Greens were critical of the 'narrow nationalism' offered by the SNP and the party's decision to have an independent Scotland remain in NATO, and articulated the party as failing to protect Scots against Tory cuts and as a friend to the oil industry. The SSP was concerned that the SNP was underplaying independence, with the SNP's policy of keeping the British monarchy as head of state having a negative effect here. Indeed, breaking down British Imperialism was a key component of the SSP's referendum campaign. The Radical Independence Campaign embodied several, if not all of these concerns about the SNP's vision of independence. However, whilst these organisation's widened the Yes coalition significantly in relation to political discourse and made it less SNP-like, they were limited by their restricted size and political reach as relatively small parties and groups, with limited memberships, resources and electorates.

Bibliography

Baird, S. and R. Harper (2005), *People, Planet, Peace: An Introduction to the Scottish Green Party*, Edinburgh, Scottish Green Party.

Bennie, L. (2004), *Understanding Political Participation: Green Party Membership in Scotland*, Farnham, Ashgate Publishing Limited.

Bennie, L. (2002), 'Exploiting New Electoral Opportunities: The Small Parties in Scotland', in Gerry Hassan and Chris Warhurst [Eds], *Tomorrow's Scotland*, London, Lawrence and Wishart.

BBC News Scotland (6th October, 2012). 'Scottish Independence:

Greens join Yes Scotland Campaign', accessed on 24th July 2013 at http://www.bbc.co.uk/news/uk-scotland-19858857.

Clegg, D. (13th November 2012). 'Ex-Labour man says Scots independence would mean new lease of life for former party', in *Daily Record*, accessed on 29th July at http://www.dailyrecord.co.uk/news/politics/dennis-canavan-says-scots-independence-1433167.

Communist Party of Scotland [2013], *A Nation Once Again?*, Glasgow, Communist Party of Scotland.

Cornock, E. (2013), 'A Marxist case for independence', article on SSP website at http://www.scottishsocialistparty.org/a-marxist-case-for-independence/

De Vreese, C. and H. Sementko, (2004), *Political Campaigning in Referendums*, New York, Routledge.

Foster, John and Richard Leonard [2013], 'Introduction', in Pauline Bryan and Tommy Kane [Eds], *Class, Nation and Socialism: The Red Paper on Scotland 2014*, Glasgow, Glasgow Caledonian University Archives.

Fox, C. (3rd June 2013), 'Independence one year nearer', accessed on 29th July 2013 via Colin Fox's blog at: http://sspcolinfox.blogspot.co.uk/search/label/Independence%20Referendum

Gonzalez, M. [2006], 'The Split in the Scottish Socialist Party', *International Socialism: A quarterly Journal of Socialist Theory*, Issue 112.

Harvie, P (10th January, 2013), Perspective: Why a Yes voter needn't be a nationalist', on 19th July 2013 accessed via the Yes Scotland website at http://www.yesscotland.net/perspective_why_a_yes_voter_needn_t_be_a_nationalist.

Harvie, P, (27th August 2013(b)), 'An Alternative Vision', in Holyrood Magazine accessed at http://www.holyrood.com/2013/08/an-alternative-vision/.

Howarth, D. and Y. Stavrakakis (2000), 'Introducing discourse theory and political analysis' in Howarth, D, Norval, A. J, Stavrakakis, Y, (2000), *'Discourse theory and political analysis'*, Manchester University Press, p. 8.

Kane, L. (2007), 'The educational influences on active citizens: A case study of members of the Scottish Socialist Party (SSP)', *Studies in the Education of Adults*, Vol. 39, No.1.

Kuin, I. (2006), 'Review: Green Party Membership', *Scottish Affairs*, No. 55, Spring, pp.138-141.

Radical Independence Campaign [2012], *Declaration for Independence*, http://radicalindependence.org/index.php/2012/11/26/declaration-for-radical-independence/.

Scottish Green Party [2012], *The Scottish Green Party Manifesto for Local Elections*, Edinburgh, Scottish Green Party.

Scottish Green Party [2010], *Westminster manifesto*, Edinburgh, Scottish Green Party.

Scottish Green Party [1999], *Caring for Scotland: An introduction to the Scottish Green Party*, Edinburgh: Scottish Green Party.

Scottish Left Review [2012], *Independence Special*, issue 73, November/December, Glasgow, Scottish Left Review.

Scottish Socialist Party [2013], *The Case for an Independent Socialist Scotland*, Glasgow, Scottish Socialist Party.

Scottish Socialist Party [2011], *Holyrood Election Manifesto*, Glasgow: Scottish Socialist Party.

Stavrakakis, Y. (2000), 'On the emergence of Green ideology: The dislocation factor in Green politics', in Howarth, D, Norval, A. J, and Stavrakakis, Y, (Eds], *Discourse theory and political analysis*, Manchester, Manchester University Press.

Notes

1. The cost of contesting a FPTP seat was £500 per seat compared to the same amount for a set of candidates on the regional list: part of the reason for the Greens contesting in regions alone. The SSP contested both then faced the expense of large losses of deposits in the FPTP contests.
2. Scottish Green Party, *Statement of Accounts*, 31st December 2012.
3. Interview with Patrick Harvie MSP, 27th August 2013.
4. Interview with Patrick Harvie MSP, 27th August 2013.
5. For discussion of this controversy see here: Gregor Gall [2012], *Tommy Sheridan: From Hero to Zero? A Political Biography*, Cardiff, Welsh Academic Press.
6. Interview with Edward Cornock and Colin Fox, 1st August 2013.
7. Compare this to 2003, when the SSP won 117,709 votes in the constituencies and 128,026 on the regional lists and you can see how far the far left had declined within 8 years.
8. Interview with Edward Cornock and Colin Fox, 1st August 2013.
9. Interview with Edward Cornock and Colin Fox, 1st August 2013.
10. This was a crowdfunding exercise through indiegogo that raised £1,565.
11. Interview with Patrick Harvie MSP, 27th August 2013.
12. Interview with Edward Cornock and Colin Fox, 1st August 2013.

8

Conclusion: Scottish Political Parties and the 2014 Independence Referendum

Kevin Adamson and Peter Lynch

Introduction

This volume was written in the mid-point of the referendum campaign, mostly over the late summer and early autumn of 2013. It was completed in a period in which the parties and referendum campaign groups were a substantial way into Scotland's longest political campaign. The Scottish Government's White Paper *Scotland's Future* [Scottish Government 2013] was published after this in November 2013 and campaigning ratcheted up several notches around this time and afterwards into 2014. However, quite a lot can be gleaned about the referendum campaign from the period before *Scotland's Future* was launched. All parties were engaged in the debate and the campaign in 2013, with parliamentary debates, publication of government studies, media and social media campaigning and on the ground campaigning and organization. All of these things were in place before the Scottish Government published its prospectus. Both Better Together and Yes Scotland had established central offices, local organizations and substantial social media presences. Local activists were involved in leafleting, distributing newspapers, information stalls and other forms of soft campaigning. Some of this was clustered around national campaign days or special events like the launch of *Scotland's Future* on 26th November 2013, when rival teams distributed campaign materials at rail stations across Scotland. Harder campaigning had also begun by the time of *Scotland's Future*, with the use of 'blether together',[1] a phone canvassing device used by Better Together and Yes Scotland's Yesmo voter database and phone canvassing network, to complement traditional doorstep canvassing. All of these things were up and running in 2013, almost a year before the referendum was to be held. In addition, it was possible to identify both the outlines and details of political discourse around the referendum issue and the various subject positions around independence, the union, welfare, governance, etc., with political parties developing their discursive strategies in light of the referendum challenge. As we have seen in this volume, the referendum allowed the Liberal Democrats to elevate federalism in their discourse, whilst parties like the Greens and Scottish Socialists produced more radical and transformative discourses around the notion radical independence.

The Economic and Political Context of the Referendum

Though the real starting gun for the independence referendum was fired with the SNP's election victory at the Scottish election of May 2011, the campaign proper did not begin until the launch of Yes Scotland and Better Together in May and June 2012. Even then, some of the campaigning took time to develop. Yes Scotland was more adept at organizing local campaigning and began early, whilst Better Together focused on monthly national campaign days and lighter campaigning as well as use of the traditional media. However, the political and economic contexts of the start of the campaign changed over time: an inevitable outcome for a long referendum campaign. Referendums, like elections, can be influenced by 'shaping events', with campaigners looking to produce the 'winning conditions' for success [former Quebec Premier Lucien Bouchard used this phrase in the context of the 1995 Sovereignty vote]. Such factors were evident in previous referendums – such as the 1979 and 1997 devolution referendums, when economic and political factors and conditions proved influential in the shape of the winter of discontent in 1978-9 and the effect of 18 years of Conservative Government on the 1997 referendum.

The 2014 independence referendum was held following one of the most turbulent economic periods in the UK's recent history. It coincided with recession and austerity across most European states, accompanied by high unemployment, bank failures, government spending cuts and widespread economic uncertainty. The effective nationalization of HBOS and Royal Bank of Scotland by the UK Government underlined the seriousness of the problems for the UK and Scottish economies. There was also public skepticism about political institutions and the political classes generally following the scandals over MPs' expenses and the performance of successive UK governments. The economic context for constitutional change was therefore highly negative, though an improving one as the referendum campaign moved into 2014. In May 2011, when the SNP government was re-elected under majority conditions, unemployment stood at 7.7 per cent, rising to 8.6 per cent in November 2011. By November 2013, Scottish unemployment stood at 6.4 percent, whereas the UK figure was 7.1 per cent.[2] Economic growth was relatively flat throughout the referendum period, with the UK in recession on several occasions during this period. However, Scottish GDP was 0.7 per cent in the third quarter of 2013,[3] whilst UK GDP grew by 0.7 per cent in the fourth quarter of 2013.[4] Interest rates remained unchanged at 0.5 per cent at the time of writing, with the consumer price index measure of inflation falling from 5.2 per cent in September 2011 to 2 per cent in December 2013. It was against this backdrop that Scottish voters were to make decision about future economic performance, currency, regulatory arrangements, tax and spending, etc., at the referendum, with an improving Scottish and UK economic picture following the Great Financial Crisis. And, certainly an improving picture compared to many other European countries during the crisis in terms of both Scottish and UK measures, which fed into the debate over independence versus the Union.

The political environment during the period of the referendum was also a changing one, though with some aspects of stability. For example, the SNP government remained popular throughout the period from the May 2011 election into early 2014, leading in most Scottish parliament polls, except from a few outliers in the autumn of 2013.[5] At the UK level, Labour maintained a narrow lead over the Conservatives. In May 2011, Labour was at 37 per cent to 36 per cent for the Conservatives.[6] In January 2014, the figures were 35 per cent to Labour and 32 per cent to the Conservatives.[7] These particular figures mattered as the prospects of future Labour/Conservative electoral success was an important conditioning factor at the referendum given the unpopularity of the Conservatives in Scotland and their role as a recruiting tool for the Yes campaign [especially amongst Labour voters]. Not dissimilar was the impact of UKIP, which was popular in the UK but not in Scotland [it is notable that UKIP was not part of Better Together]. It had registered lost deposits in Scottish parliament by-elections and limited opinion poll ratings. Yet at the UK level [meaning England and Wales here really], it was capable of winning support but not seats at by-elections, winning local council seats and registering 17 per cent in opinion polls.[8] Its rise played into a Yes narrative about Scotland and the UK having different political cultures and moving in different directions. In terms of opinion polling on independence, almost all polls were negative for Yes. Just before the Scottish election of May 2011, a Yougov poll for *The Scotsman*, found 28 per cent would vote Yes, compared to 57 per cent No and 15 per cent don't know.[9] No led in polls throughout, if there was a Yes-No question, though there were occasional Yes leads on contextual questions.[10] At the time of writing, a ICM poll for Scotland on Sunday reported that the Yes-No gap had narrowed, with Yes on 37 per cent to No on 44 per cent, with don't knows at 19 per cent.[11] In addition, though the referendum was ostensibly about Scottish independence, the nature of the issue and the duration of the campaign meant it became linked to a wide range of other issues in Scottish and UK politics. Issues like the spare room subsidy/bedroom tax, immigration policy, Scottish and UK membership of the European Union [with Conservative enthusiasm for a Brexit referendum], austerity measures, levels of corporate taxation and tax avoidance and a myriad of other issues related to independence and to politics and economics generally. The issue scope for campaigning and for pressure groups and civic organizations was therefore extremely broad.

The Parties and the Referendum

In chapter 1, we identified five factors that made political parties central to the referendum campaign: their role as organizations that would provide campaign finance, personnel and resources, the office benefits available to parties to influence the referendum, the role of political parties as producers of political discourse, the capacity of parties to shape the political landscape through policies, debates and positions and finally, the manner in which parties offer political cues to voters over referendum questions. All of these aspects of party influence were observable during the referendum campaign, though not equally shared by all of the parties. Moreover, they existed despite academic research on the decline of political parties and levels of partisanship across Western democracies where there was a tendency to ask 'do parties matter?' and answer in the negative with Mair going as far to argue that about party decline leading to the hollowing out of democracy [Mair 2013]. In the case of the Scottish independence referendum parties clearly did matter in all sorts of ways and some of them were already growing as organisations before the referendum [in the case of the SNP] and during it the case of the Greens and SSP and also perhaps the Conservatives. How prevalent this was across the political parties remains to be seen though, as we shall see, campaigning has come to involve not just party members but a looser group of party supporters and in the case of the referendum, volunteers from outside the parties: which was the explicit intention of both Better Together and Yes Scotland.

The SNP was central to the Yes campaign and the prospects for a Yes vote in 2014 at all levels though sensitive of the need to make Yes Scotland cross-party and to involve a wide range of people in the campaign. The party drove the referendum issue and its organization, resources, activists and government were key actors at all levels. In terms of campaigning, discourse, strategy and planning, the details of independence [all those Scottish Government papers as well as the White Paper itself], the parliamentary legislation for the referendum, policies, ideas, etc., the SNP was vitally important. The SNP was not immune to external influences though, hence the links to the Common Weal agenda evident in the White Paper. Despite all this, the SNP's position was a difficult one. Relations with Yes Scotland were tense at times, given the different roles and experiences of the two organizations – not least in relation to fighting elections though the transfer of SNP elections staff to Yes in late 2013 aided this problem. Furthermore, like all the other political parties, the SNP had party interests to consider in relation to policy, elections and government as the referendum was one of a sequence of electoral events from 2014-16. The central role of the SNP and Alex Salmond were also difficult issues for the party during the referendum as the party's opponents sought to target Salmond personally to damage independence. Scottish politics is a very tribal world and the SNP had to deal with that reality through projecting its party interests at the same time as providing political space for competitors like the Greens, Labour for Independence and the Scottish Socialist Party, with their very different political campaigning styles and party cultures.

For Labour, the referendum was an existential threat but also an opportunity to strike back at the SNP in order seek to derail the party that had so comprehensively replaced it at the 2011 Scottish election. With careful handling, the referendum was an opportunity to inflict a defeat on the SNP's very raison d'etre and perhaps undermine its leader Alex Salmond. However, Labour faced difficulties here in a number of ways. First, it had a great deal to lose from the referendum at the Scottish and UK levels but had to adopt a leadership role at the referendum as the largest pro-Union party and the only one with any political credibility. This role was compromised by the need to cooperate with the Conservatives and Liberal Democrats in an ideologically incoherent No campaign. The fact that Better Together was largely financed by Conservative supporters did not help. Labour's response was to cooperate with Better Together but set up its own separate campaign group United with Labour to insulate itself from the Conservatives and also provide a mechanism to encourage Labour members and the trade unions to play a role in the campaign. However, as Eric Shaw's chapter demonstrated, some major trade unions were reluctant to become involved in the No campaign. Second, it was clear from the launch of Yes Scotland in May 2012 that a lot of the positions advanced by Yes Scotland were directed towards Labour voters. Yes sought to attract support from Labour figures and members to demonstrate that independence was popular beyond the SNP and broaden the Yes coalition. Whilst the Scottish political left had moved towards independence with the Radical independence movement contesting this political space with the much-smaller Red Paper Collective, the launch of Labour for Independence in 2012 brought the independence challenge to within the Labour Party membership and by extension, the Labour electorate. After a slow start, Labour for Independence began to develop a stronger profile, aided by support from former major Labour figures like former council leaders Charles Gray, Alex Mosson and John Mulvey in 2013.[12] Third, the devolution issue remained problematic for Labour internally with public divisions on what 'offer' Scottish Labour should make on increased devolution in advance of the independence referendum [Macintosh, The Herald, 3rd February 2014].

Whilst the independence referendum brought a challenge to the existential Unionism of the Conservatives, the event was actually helpful to galvanize a faltering political party. Scottish Conservativism had struggled for several decades after 1979, notably with complete electoral collapse in 1997. Devolution, paradoxically, had helped restore the Conservatives as an electoral force in Scotland but the party failed to make much impact at UK general elections nonetheless. Post-2011, the party struggled with the devolution reform issue before deciding to examine its devolution policy through a party commission set to report before the referendum in September 2014. However, in other respects, the referendum issue was positive for the party. It gave it something to concentrate on and obviously, something to attack, which united its MSPs, party members and supporters after a fractious period. The result was that in the short term, the party grew and was able to raise funds.

The referendum was an interesting political challenge for the Liberal Democrats in Scotland. The party's participation in the UK coalition government in 2010 proved catastrophic for the party's electoral performance at the Scottish election of 2011 and the local council elections in 2012. Party membership had slipped considerably along with representation and the party faced a major challenge to retain its Westminster seats in Scotland at the 2015 UK general election. Despite adopting a defensive posture in campaigning to bolster its incumbent MPs, the party did develop something more distinctive for the referendum campaign in the shape of a 'federalist' discourse in arguing for more devolved powers, localism and a federal UK. This discourse was evident in the party's Steel Commission report in 2006 and Home Rule Commission in 2012 but became a feature of its campaign discourse throughout the middle phase of the independence referendum. It did offer a distinctive position in the overall debate – which was often focused on 'more powers' options – but also helped the party to rediscover its Scottish face given the unpopularity of the coalition government.

For the smaller parties like the Greens and Scottish Socialists, the independence referendum was a considerable opportunity, though perhaps not one they were fully able to capitalize on given their size, organisation and resources. As part of the Yes coalition, the smaller parties had a new relevance. They were able to promote their own issue agendas through the independence issue to gain new audiences and, in the specific case of the SSP, to rebuild following recent traumas from 2003-7. Issues around energy or welfare reform were knitted into arguments over autonomy, independence and power in society and participation in Yes events brought activists and leaders to greater prominence. How much these parties learned from the referendum in terms of organization, strategy and planning was a moot point however, limiting their future development and capacities.

Of course, party activity at the campaign level has become differentiated in recent years. On the one hand, party memberships have generally fallen across the piece in the UK in recent years though membership has grown steadily in the case of the SNP and there were signs of 'referendum effects' in relation to membership growth amongst the Greens and SSP [though from a low base]. Whether the Conservatives, Labour and Liberal Democrats see similar membership growth due to political mobilisation during the referendum campaign is an open question. However, formal party membership is not the only measure of election campaigning and is directly relevant to the referendum and the organizational logics of Better Together and Yes Scotland. Studies from the UK general of 2010 identified the growth in campaign activity of party supporters at elections, with local parties seeing activity from supporters who were not formal members of the party [Fisher, Fieldhouse and Cutts, 2014]. The study saw campaigning by supporters in 86 per cent of Liberal Democrat campaigns and 75 per cent of both Conservative and Labour campaigns locally [*Ibid.*, p.80]. Supporters were active in some numbers – with means of 22 for the

Conservatives, 19 for the Liberal Democrats and 13 for Labour in each local party – though supporters were not as active as party members and involved more in leafleting and polling day work than more complex campaign activities like doorstep and telephone canvassing [*Ibid*: 83]. Two conclusions can be drawn from this study. First, on the one hand it points to the fact that viewing party membership as a 'hard' measure of support for a party has its flaws as it underestimates the existence of 'supporters' and the fact that they do supplement the work of members quite considerably when it comes to political campaigning at the coalface come election time. Therefore, we are looking at larger numbers of active campaigners than just the party members. Second, when you transpose this onto the referendum, with its loose umbrella groups, soft campaigning activities and volunteer ethos you can see how it gelled with the need to attract party members, party supporters but also completely new volunteers and activists. How many of the latter category become mobilized and active in politics – and continue their activity after the referendum is an interesting question for the future of political participation in Scotland.

Political Parties and Referendum Discourse: Mapping the Terrain

Although the authors of the chapters on parties in this volume make clear that party strategies are distinctive in terms of the campaign, in terms of structure the terrain, perhaps unsurprisingly, is divided by a fairly clear political frontier. The Yes/No nature of the debate imposes its own constraints on how innovative parties on each side could be in terms of discursive strategy. On a basic level, the parties were free to construct their own meaning for the two most important empty signifiers in the debate, 'Yes', and 'No'. But the emergence of fairly unified umbrella campaigns on both sides of the divide led to important similarities in the structure of discourses emanating from parties within the respective campaigns. The three main parties of the No campaign coalesced around a positive discourse that broadly defended the Union through the promotion of the theme of common British identity, while attempting to put to one side their differences in terms of public policy, particularly in the case of the Conservatives and the Liberal Democrats in relation to Labour [which all contrasted starkly with the level of policy differences and conflict in the parallel world of Westminster party competition during the referendum campaign].

On the negative side, the three No parties concentrated on articulating numerous 'unanswered questions' about independence, which long term has attempted to build an equivalence between two empty signifiers, 'independence' and 'uncertainty' (or sometimes 'risk'). There was also evidence of coalescence between the No parties with regard to the constitution of the United Kingdom. Typically, for Labour and the Liberal Democrats, 'devolution' as a signifier sat comfortably within their wider respective discourses on the Union, with the Liberal Democrats, as noted by Harvey in chapter 6, articulating devolution as part of wider proposals for federalism within the UK, while Labour articulated 'devolution' as one of the major constitutional achievements of their party, both for Scotland and the United Kingdom. Although, as noted by Torrance [chapter 5], the Conservatives campaigned against devolution in 1997, they have participated since then in the Scottish Parliament and have also come more recently to articulate 'devolution' within a positive chain of equivalence that included the Union, which is probably the most interesting ideological development among the No parties. The most important empty signifier for the No parties was 'Britain', and it served as something that could be positively articulated in discourse in strong relation with 'British' and 'Britishness'. The discursive unity of the No campaign parties was mostly built around this. At the same time, the detail of the policy direction of the United Kingdom was a source of daily political contestation between these parties, particularly between Labour and the coalition of Conservatives and Liberal Democrats. This resulted, as noted by Shaw [chapter 4], in the establishment of separate campaign initiatives from Labour, and divergent narratives about the future of Britain. This development occurred despite the fact that all of the No parties sought to place the production of discourse in favour of No above party competition over policy details [as if 'normal' politics could be suspended in Scotland during the referendum, but continue at the UK level without anyone noticing].

For the Yes campaign, policy differences between the parties were actively articulated as a central positive element of Yes discourse and the parties' own discourses supporting independence. This was tied to their narrative of what would happen with independence, that following a Yes vote there would be fresh elections in 2016 at which the political parties would compete for votes, the outcome of which would decide the future policy directions of Scotland. This narrative may seem banal, but it was a central plank of the Yes campaign's discourse, that the issue being decided by the referendum was also beyond, or above, party competition. The Yes campaign also saw a proliferation of activity from two smaller parties, the Greens (with two MSPs 2011-16] and the Scottish Socialist Party (who have had no MSPs since 2007), as well as other associated campaigns on the radical left, in particular the Common Weal Project, and the Radical Independence Conference. Gillen's contribution in chapter 7 looked at the Greens and the SSP and identified and analyzed their radical contribution to the discourses of the referendum. The unifying theme of the radical parties was 'democracy' in Scotland, that an independent Scotland would be more democratic – which converged with one major Yes Scotland narrative that Scotland should get the government it votes for [an argument about Conservative illegitimacy in Scotland that goes back to the Doomsday Scenario of the mid-1980s]. For the Greens, independence would create greater possibilities for 'environmental sustainability', while for the Socialists it would produce real opportunities for 'social justice' and 'socialist' policies. While these two parties are clearly electoral opponents of the SNP, their articulation of 'independence', though cast in radical terms, was ideologically proximate to some of the main signifiers used by the SNP to articulate the meaning of independence. This allowed for a relatively coherent, and policy-thick, discourse on the meaning of independence to be articulated on behalf of the Yes campaign that contrasted with the ideological divergence and policy-free nature of the No campaign.

If we consider the two most important political parties in the referendum – the SNP and Labour – it is clear that the frontier dividing these parties accounted for the majority of the discursive production of the campaign from the actors involved. In terms of Scottish politics, they are direct electoral competitors, both seeking governing majorities at Holyrood. Part of the SNP's discursive strategy since its election victory in 2007 was to present itself as a competent governing party, albeit within the parameters of a limited, devolution-constrained political and financial settlement: itself an opportunity for discursive production around arguments for more powers. Within the period of the referendum campaign, this discursive strategy was modified to articulate Scotland's governability, on the back of two terms of 'competence' in office and to build independence on the 'successes' of devolution in policy and governance. In response, the Labour Party sought to contest the 'competence' of the SNP government and the First Minister in particular, while also seeking to articulate an 'equivalence' between 'independence' and 'Alex Salmond'. Within this discursive battle, SNP discourse moved through several stages to articulate firstly 'could' Scotland be independent, to 'should' be independent, and also to present a wide ranging depiction of what an independent Scotland might look like. This strategy culminated in the publication in November 2013 of the Scottish Government's White Paper, *Scotland's Future*. The UK Government also produced reports and studies that were used mainly by the No campaign and rearticulated in the No campaign by the Labour Party. Part of the distinctively Scottish Labour discursive strategy was to use the referendum campaign to cast doubt over the claims for independence made by the SNP Government, with a particular focus on contesting the SNP's articulation of 'independence' and 'social justice'. The SNP's strategy to concentrate on articulating independence with 'social justice' and democracy helped to support the ideological coherence of the Yes campaign. But as Alex Salmond claimed that Scotland could become a 'progressive beacon', this position also presented a serious challenge to the Labour Party as the two parties contested the social democratic space in Scotland through debates on policy, policy delivery, universalism and political values. In responding to this challenge, Johann Lamont, leader of the Labour Party in Scotland, led the charges that the SNP's social democratic promises were unsustainable, and claimed that 'Scotland cannot be the only "something for nothing" culture.' All intended with the dual purpose of challenging the SNP government over ideology and delivery as well as over the prospectus for independence: intended to challenge Labour's main competitor, prevent Labour voters from defecting to the SNP and to Yes in 2014 and assist Labour's electoral prospects at the 2015 UK general election and 2016 Scottish election.

The Emergence of Non-Party Actors

Whilst political parties were central actors in the campaign and their role important in relation to the outcome of the referendum, other political actors did emerge and there was a more general level of engagement with a large number of political and economic issues from social organizations and pressure groups in relation to the independence referendum. Most of the engagement in relation to campaigning seemed to have come on the Yes side of the referendum, with new organizations formed like Radical Independence, National Collective and the Common Weal organization. There were a number of interesting aspects to these groups. First, in conventional political science terms, they were difficult to classify. The new organizations existed somewhere between social movements and think tanks and involved a range of individuals and perspectives. Radical Independence began as a conference before becoming a campaign with a loose organization around Scotland. It attracted supporters, discussed policy and political ideas, acted as a formal campaigning organization and yet remained a loose network of individuals from the Greens, SNP, SSP, community activists, trade unions and social groups. In campaigning terms its public face was limited compared to Yes Scotland – in terms of formal election-type campaigning, numbers and activities – but it did address different audiences and make the Yes campaign a broader political and social force on the left.

The National Collective was a different case entirely, as it embraced the cultural and creative spheres in Scotland taking in art, design, filmmaking, literature, music, etc. Its activities involved running its own events, website and social media campaign to reach a different audience. The Common Weal organization was established by the Reid Foundation [a left of centre thank tank created in the pre-referendum period]. The Common Weal sought to build a network of ideas, policies and people to offer a progressive vision for Scotland, to escape the individualism and consumerism of the past thirty years. Along with the Reid Foundation, it became a generator of policy ideas and discussion across the centre-left in Scotland with a strong media profile.

Crowdfunding was central to many of the activities of non-party actors – as most lacked institutional forms of support and/or strong existing networks of supporters. Crowdfunding was used to finance campaigning, staff resources and media efforts during the referendum by a range of organizations. For example, Radical Scotland, National Collective, Bella Caledonia and the Common Weal were just some of the organisations to use crowdfunding sites like indiegogo to raise money for their activities. Indiegogo was a crowdfunding platform which political organizations could use to raise specific amounts of money over a limited timeframe, with the funding campaign promoted through social media. Facebook sharing and use of twitter by supporters would bring the financial appeal to a wider audience – for free – and supporters would gain a range of benefits from contributing in terms of badges, t-shirts, campaign packs, etc. In this way, new political organizations were able to raise reasonable sums of money through small donations from a wide range of individuals. The level of funding here was vastly inferior to the amounts raised by Yes Scotland and

Table 8.1 Crowdfunding for Non-Party Actors 2013.

Organization	Amount	Platform
Bella Caledonia	£13,480	Indiegogo
Common Weal	£25,585	Indiegogo
National Collective	£18,360	Indiegogo
Newsnet Scotland	£13,801	Indiegogo
Radical Independence	£2,082	Indiegogo

Source: Indiegogo appeals data.

Better Together but then their activities and scope were quite different too – meaning much more limited. However, what was significant was that they developed and mushroomed in the period leading up to the referendum as part of a wider mobilization.

A final new development associated with the referendum campaign involved the development of a new media, using social media, blogging and online new sites. Much of the traditional media – particularly the newspapers – were aligned with the No campaign and some operated effectively as No campaign newspapers with regular front page lead stories on the negatives of independence. Neither Yes Scotland nor the broader Yes campaign could compete with this structural disadvantage directly but sought to compensate through developing its own media. This development was already underway before the referendum campaign began but mushroomed during the campaign as an unofficial media began to grow to challenge the official media of broadcasting and newspapers. Three good examples were Bella Caledonia, Newsnet Scotland and Wings over Scotland, though many other websites provided political analysis and journalistic commentaries too. Bella Caledonia was launched as an online magazine in 2007, run on a voluntary basis with a range of contributors from a range of political perspectives related to independence. Newsnet Scotland was launched in 2010 to provide a more balanced media – meaning more pro-SNP and pro-independence. It developed through the work of volunteers and then fundraising appeals [£13,801 via indiegogo in 2013] and regular donations through its website. Wings over Scotland was launched in 2011 as a pro-independence blog by a former Liberal Democrat voter Stuart Campbell. This website was prepared to be much more controversial than other online campaigners with use of humour and targeting of opponents. The relevance and impact of these new media outlets is difficult to discern. They produced their own journalism in terms of stories, opinion, cartoons, commissioned pieces, political and cultural coverage and also the sharing of stories via social media [their own stories and a wide range of others]. So, besides existing as media outlets they are also networking, sharing and community sites. The question is whether they compete with traditional media outlets [which also have their own social media sharing mechanisms]. There's no easy answer to this but then the monthly views of these news sites do compare reasonably well with some newspaper sales in Scotland. Newsnet Scotland was averaging 12,000 visits a day into November 2013. Bella Caledonia gained 347,000 page views in October 2013 and Wings over Scotland had 708,019 unique visitors to its site in 2013 and over 16 million page views. [13]Compare this with daily sales figures of 31,300 for The Scotsman, 41,000 for The Herald and 65,500 for the

Press and Journal and you can see the importance of the growth of the pro-independence news sites, though the online versions of these Scottish papers was growing at the same time as their paper versions were losing sales.[14] One way of understanding what was going on was that Yes supporters at all levels were using social media to build a pro-Yes media where none existed and to reduce the political effects of the pro-Union newspapers in particular by providing alternative news sources and commentary.

Conclusion

There are three sets of conclusions we can draw about the role and functions of political parties in the context of the independence referendum. First, that the referendum campaign pointed to the continued relevance of political parties as key actors in all levels of political activity in the campaign. Despite signs of organizational decline and declining levels of partisanship, the Scottish party scene demonstrated signs of growth before and during the referendum campaign, especially amongst those parties active in Yes Scotland. Regardless of growth, the parties were key actors in government, campaigning, research, finance, personnel, activists, etc., across all aspects of the referendum. They were not the sole actors as the discussion above in relation to crowd-funded social organisations illustrates, but they were the most prominent. Second, the parties themselves were major actors in producing and promoting political discourse around the referendum and a range of contested concepts and empty signifiers around independence, the Union, welfare, social justice, etc. The parties and umbrella campaign groups had clear discursive strategies to implement during the campaign, as they contested the meaning of ideas and understandings of the core issues in the referendum. Third, the effect of the parties on the referendum campaign and outcome was a moot point in this study, as it captured part but not all of the referendum campaign. Parties are central to campaigns but it was a question whether they really affected campaign outcomes either through their ground or air wars in either the short or long campaign around the referendum and how much political campaigns actually matter in shaping the electoral outcomes.

Bibliography

Fisher, J. and Denver, D. (2009), 'Evaluating the electoral effects of traditional and modern modes of constituency campaigning in Britain 1992–2005', *Parliamentary Affairs*, Vol. 62:2, pp.196–210.

Fisher, J., E. Fieldhouse and D. Cutts [2014], 'Members Are Not the Only Fruit: Volunteer Activity in British Political Parties at the 2010 General Election', *British Journal of Politics and International Relations*, Vol. 16, pp. 75–95.

Macintosh, Ken (2014), Agenda, The Herald, 3rd February 2014, http://www.heraldscotland.com/comment/columnists/agenda.23314079

Mair, Peter [2013], *Ruling the Void: The Hollowing of Western Democracy*, London, Verso.

Scottish Government [2013], *Scotland's Future*, Edinburgh, Scottish Government.

Notes

1. See video explanation on youtube here - http://www.youtube.com/watch?v=So6X5UUnEUs&feature=c4-overview&list=UUKTXq91LTofxlv98ZS8TfbQ
2. Office for National Statistics, *Unemployment Rate for Government Office Region*, at http://www.ons.gov.uk/ons/interactive/unemployment-rate-by-region---dvc7/index.html
3. Scottish Government statistical Bulletin, 15th January 2014, at Scottish GDP -http://www.scotland.gov.uk/Resource/0044/00441866.pdf
4. Office of National Statistics, 28th January 2014, at http://www.ons.gov.uk/ons/dcp171780_350942.pdf .
5. http://whatscotlandthinks.org/questions/how-would-you-use-your-constituency-vote-in-a-scottish-parliament-election#line
6. ICM in The Guardian, 3rd May 2011,
7. ICM in The Guardian, 12th January 2014.
8. Opinium poll in The Observer, 4th January 2014.
9. The Scotsman, 28th April 2011.
10. See for example, John Curtice, *The Score at Half-time* at http://www.scotcen.org.uk/media/270726/SSA-13-The-Score-At-Half-Time.pdf
11. Scotland on Sunday, 24th January 2014.
12. See www.labourforindy.com
13. http://wingsoverscotland.com/wp content/uploads/2014/01/2013statstotal.jpg
14. http://www.bbc.co.uk/news/uk-scotland-scotland-business-23873955.